*"This readable, accessible text integrates biblical studies and contemporary psychology to address the issue of a personal Christian authenticity in our time. Troy Watson's generous use of story and illustration provides constant clarity as he addresses the individual challenge of living before God in Christ by the power of the Holy Spirit."*

**TEX SAMPLE**, Robert B. and Kathleen Rogers Professor Emeritus of Church and Society at the Saint Paul School of Theology and author of *Micro Practices for Justice Ministry: Doing Little Things for the Common Good*

*"Filled with pastoral wisdom and underlined with theological insight, this wonderfully accessible book is a trustworthy guide on the journey of healthy, holistic spiritual formation. Troy Watson has crafted a gift for all who want to understand themselves, and their identity in Christ, better, and so understand the beautiful, paradoxical, authentic selves God created them to be."*

**MICHAEL PAHL**, executive minister of Mennonite Church Manitoba and author of *The Word Fulfilled: Reading the Bible with Jesus*

*"What a perfectly timed book for our generation! Troy Watson has provided those of us working with young adults a highly accessible resource for helping them navigate struggles with self-worth and identity. This book is not only valuable for my own growth as a pastor but is also an excellent option for small groups. Thank you, Troy, for offering fresh insights into an age-old challenge, and for encouraging us to trust in God's affirmation of who we are, rather than the world's. This book is a timely and powerful reminder of where true identity and worth are found."*

**NICK LADD**, campus pastor and Bible professor at Hesston College

*"Troy Watson's words of care a ... with story-*
*telling and humor, invite you t ... fe,*
*the blind spots and the crack ...*
*ignore, in order to allow for d ... y*
*to allow for the truest versior ...*
*hope for the world."*

**BETTY PRIES**, cofounder and CEO of Credence & Co. and author ... *pace Between Us*, from the foreword

# Get a Hold of Yourself

# GET A HOLD OF YOURSELF

## EMBRACING AUTHENTICITY IN A COMPLICATED WORLD

**TROY D. WATSON**

FOREWORD BY BETTY PRIES

**HERALD PRESS**

Harrisonburg, Virginia

Herald Press
PO Box 866, Harrisonburg, Virginia 22803
www.HeraldPress.com

Library of Congress Cataloging-in-Publication Data applied for.

Study guides are available for many Herald Press titles at www.HeraldPress.com.

GET A HOLD OF YOURSELF
© 2025 by Herald Press, Harrisonburg, Virginia 22803. 800-245-7894. All rights reserved.
Library of Congress Control Number: 2025011265
International Standard Book Number: 978-1-5138-1643-2 (paperback);
    978-1-5138-1645-6 (ebook)
Printed in United States of America

All rights reserved. This publication may not be reproduced, stored in a retrieval system, or transmitted in whole or in part, in any form, by any means, electronic, mechanical, photo-copying, recording or otherwise without prior permission of the copyright owners.

All scripture quotations, unless otherwise indicated, are taken from the Holy Bible, New International Version®, NIV®. Copyright © 1973, 1978, 1984, 2011 by Biblica, Inc.® Used by permission of Zondervan. All rights reserved worldwide. www.zondervan.com. The "NIV" and "New International Version" are trademarks registered in the United States Patent and Trademark Office by Biblica, Inc.®

Scripture quotations marked (NLT) are taken from the Holy Bible, New Living Translation, copyright © 1996, 2004, 2015 by Tyndale House Foundation. Used by permission of Tyndale House Publishers, Inc., Carol Stream, Illinois 60188. All rights reserved.

Scripture quotations marked (NRSVue) are taken from the New Revised Standard Version Updated Edition. Copyright © 2021 National Council of Churches of Christ in the United States of America. Used by permission. All rights reserved worldwide.

29 28 27 26 25          10 9 8 7 6 5 4 3 2 1

To my Creator, who has walked patiently and graciously with me, and made this book possible. To my wife Tammy and our sons Elias and Cai. You embody the authenticity I aspire to. You are the light I'm most grateful for in this life. To my parents, brothers, in-laws, family, friends, mentors, sojourners . . . everyone who has touched my life and helped me grow. To all those seeking to live authentically and in harmony with the Most High. I hope this book encourages you to shine your light.

# CONTENTS

Foreword . . . . . . . . . . . . . . . . . . . . . . . . . . . . . . . 11
Introduction . . . . . . . . . . . . . . . . . . . . . . . . . . . . 13

1 **Paradox** . . . . . . . . . . . . . . . . . . . . . . . . . . . . 17
2 **Expectations** . . . . . . . . . . . . . . . . . . . . . . . . 35
3 **Desire** . . . . . . . . . . . . . . . . . . . . . . . . . . . . . 53
4 **Death** . . . . . . . . . . . . . . . . . . . . . . . . . . . . . 69
5 **Identity** . . . . . . . . . . . . . . . . . . . . . . . . . . . . 81
6 **Home** . . . . . . . . . . . . . . . . . . . . . . . . . . . . . 103
7 **Snakes** . . . . . . . . . . . . . . . . . . . . . . . . . . . . 121
8 **Self** . . . . . . . . . . . . . . . . . . . . . . . . . . . . . . 139
9 **Christ** . . . . . . . . . . . . . . . . . . . . . . . . . . . . . 159
10 **Authenticity** . . . . . . . . . . . . . . . . . . . . . . . . 175

Conclusion . . . . . . . . . . . . . . . . . . . . . . . . . . . . . 195
Notes . . . . . . . . . . . . . . . . . . . . . . . . . . . . . . . . 201
The Author . . . . . . . . . . . . . . . . . . . . . . . . . . . . 205

# FOREWORD

For many years now, I have had the privilege of reading monthly articles written by Troy Watson in the *Canadian Mennonite* magazine. I have found Troy's articles to be thoughtful, funny, introspective, and often deeply meaningful. I was delighted, then, several years ago, when I saw Troy's name on the participant list for a workshop I was teaching. Since that workshop, Troy and I have had numerous conversations, each of which has been inspiring to me.

Through the chapters of this book, Troy's numerous insights invite us to find ourselves anew even if the place that houses our deepest self feels frightening. He states, "The things you really want in life are often found in the places you least want to go. The path to the things we desire most, like freedom, peace, joy, healing, and love, usually take us down roads we'd rather not travel."

My own life's work includes, among other things, teaching workshops on topics such as communication, conflict transformation, coaching, and mediation. During workshops related to mediation and coaching, I like to say to participants, "You have to put yourself *in* the way in order to get yourself *out* of the way." If we want to be truly present to the people around us, we have to work at our own "stuff," lest we perceive others unfairly because of our own unresolved hurts, biases, and blind spots.

To lead people and processes well, Troy invites us to practice *kenosis*, a type of self-emptying ascribed to Jesus. *Kenosis* asks us to release our ego-attachments, that things must go our way, that our high or low self-esteem must be satisfied in each interaction. Ultimately, *kenosis* asks us to practice dying to our falsely constructed selves—a lifelong task—to be daily "reborn" as the unique and beautiful people we were each created to be, and to reground ourselves in the deepest truth of our being: that we are each beloved of God.

Almost as if by design, shortly after I read *Get a Hold of Yourself*, nearly every conversation with clients and friends seemed to engage the same themes as those found in this book. A coincidence? Perhaps I was simply attuned to the themes in the book and therefore noticed them as they emerged? A third possibility is just as likely—the themes were part of my conversations precisely because exploring the ideas found in this book is necessary for those thinking about what it means to be a person, those wanting to make sense of the world, and those longing to be well when in community with others. Increasingly, I find that these types of conversations have become important to the people with whom I work and play.

Troy's words of care and wisdom, interspersed with storytelling and humor, invite you to go to the tender spaces in your life, the blind spots and the cracks in your being you would prefer to ignore, in order to allow for deep healing to occur, and ultimately to allow for the truest version of yourself to become a beacon of hope for the world.

—Betty Pries

Cofounder and CEO of Credence & Co.
and author of *The Space Between Us*

# INTRODUCTION

One July several years back, I decided to see how far I could hike along the Bruce Trail in southern Ontario in three days. The first few hours were delightful, traversing through the escarpment forest, by rivers and waterfalls. But by noon, I started hitting dead ends, overgrown trails and "No Trespassing" signs. It became clear my map didn't match the trail.

I'd assumed my twelve-year-old trail map would be fine. I was wrong. I kept getting lost, having to backtrack to find the rerouted trail. Instead of wandering through fields and forest, the new route took me on extended detours along asphalt and concrete, along busy highways, on the hottest day of the summer. It eventually led me through a highly congested urban area, past the largest shopping mall in Niagara. People stared at me from their cars and city bus windows as I hobbled through downtown, covered in sweat and dust, with my gargantuan backpack, enormous sunhat and awkwardly tall "Gandalfian" hiking stick. This wasn't what I'd envisioned for my "get back to nature" hike.

With the risk of sounding like the faded motivational posters on the walls of my middle school classroom, life is like a hike. My Bruce Trail hike, that is. Sometimes our path takes us to places full of beauty, grandeur, and serenity. Other times, it leads us to places we'd rather avoid. Places we hadn't envisioned our route taking us. We hit dead ends in our careers, relationships, and life goals. We get lost and need to backtrack. Sometimes we're forced to start over. Our lives don't unfold the way we think they will. Not all the time. Sooner or later, we realize the map we're using to navigate through life no longer matches the terrain we're hiking. We realize our maps are outdated. Like I discovered at a dead end somewhere (not) on the Bruce Trail.

I've been pastoring for over twenty-six years. I've counseled and walked alongside many people, and I'm no longer surprised when people have a faith crisis. It's only a matter of time for most of us. What has surprised me is this: few of us are willing to take the inner journey required to update the maps we use to navigate our lives, especially our faith maps. We resist updating our maps, even when it's clear they're no longer working for us.

Sometimes we go to the other extreme and throw away our maps. We look for new maps. Better maps. That's what I did in my mid-twenties when I experimented with agnosticism. I explored a lot of other maps, assuming the Bible and Christianity were outdated and archaic ways of looking at the world. However, I eventually realized my old faith map didn't need to be replaced; it needed to be updated.

In my undergraduate and graduate studies, I explored theology, philosophy, Scripture, Jungian psychology, and Christian mysticism, and I made a great deal of progress in updating my old map. But there was more work to be done.

## UPDATING OUR NAVIGATION SETTINGS

One time Google Maps told me it was impossible to reach my destination. After a few minutes of confusion and frustration,

I realized I had the "Avoid Tolls" option selected. As soon as I corrected the settings, my phone said I'd arrive at my destination in shortly over an hour.

In addition to being a pastor for the past twenty-six years, I've been the director of an arts and spirituality center, a multifaith dialogue facilitator, a church planting consultant, and a columnist for a newspaper and Christian magazine. I've counseled, coached, and walked alongside many people over the past two decades, from all sorts of backgrounds, and I've learned most of us have an "Avoid This" setting turned on in our lives, that makes moving forward difficult, if not impossible.

Some of us avoid questions and doubts. Or we avoid our feelings, inner wounds, and fears. Some of us avoid conflict or taking responsibility for our lives. Some of us avoid certain personalities, political perspectives, or "heretical" schools of thought. Whatever it is, most of us have an "Avoid This" option turned on in our internal navigation system that inevitably causes us to hit a dead end or get stuck.

In hindsight, I see that every time I was stuck in life, the only way I was able to move forward was by updating my map or checking my navigation settings to see what I was avoiding.

This book is about how to update our psychological, theological, and spiritual maps and stop avoiding the things we must face to become our authentic self.

My prayer is this book will provide insight on how to develop an updated and meaningful map for your faith in the twenty-first century. I hope it will offer you fresh language and a new framework for understanding the ancient yet timeless message of Christ. Above all, I pray it will provide a new way of viewing the paradoxical contradictions in the Bible and your own life. To see them as invitations to an inner journey towards awakening and authenticity.

# 1

# PARADOX

Some friends and I were engaged in a playful debate about which one of us was the best driver. We soon began exchanging humorous stories about the spotty driving record of the one person we agreed was the worst driver. I'll call him Kenneth. His first driving incident happened a few months after getting his license, when he was sixteen years old. He backed into his brother's car, leaving a large dent in the driver door. The number of dings, scratches, and damage he's afflicted upon wildlife, stationary objects, and the vehicles of family and friends over the decades since then is remarkable.

My favorite Kenneth collision story was his five-second Segway ride at a beach resort a few summers ago. (A Segway is a self-balancing transport device you stand on and maneuver by shifting your weight.) Kenneth paid his twenty dollars, hopped on and took off at full speed, crashing into a large monument sign a few feet in front of him, ending his joyride as quickly as it began. While he walked away unscathed, the same could not be said for the sign or the Segway.

You can imagine our reaction when Kenneth claimed to be the best driver in our friend group. At first, we thought he was

18   **Get a Hold of Yourself**

joking. He wasn't. He claimed to be a better driver than all of us and at least 90 percent of drivers on the road.

Kenneth has many gifts and talents, but he has a blind spot when it comes to driving, hindering his ability to see mailboxes, trees, and parked vehicles, as well as his own dubious driving skills. We all have blind spots in our lives and overestimate ourselves in certain areas. Psychologists refer to the tendency to view ourselves as above average as the Lake Wobegon effect. Our inclination to overestimate our abilities, knowledge, or competence is called the Dunning-Kruger effect. This helps explain why Kenneth thinks he's an above average driver. He's not alone. Ninety-three percent of Americans think they're better-than-average drivers.[1] Which is, of course, statistically impossible.

A plethora of studies have revealed that most of us struggle to assess ourselves accurately, from our work performance, to our parenting knowledge, to our investing skills. In short, most of us are not as self-aware as we think we are.

In her book *Insight*, organizational psychologist and author Dr. Tasha Eurich posits that 95 percent of us claim to be self-aware, but only 10 to 15 percent of us are.[2] Although modern technology and social media have compounded our self-awareness issues, this problem isn't new. Jesus highlighted it two thousand years ago when he said that most of us are quick to see specks in other people's eyes while missing the logs in our own eyes (Matthew 7:3–5). Human beings have struggled with self-awareness throughout history, across all cultures, since the beginning of time. It's the human condition.

Thankfully, there's hope.

Twelve-step programs inform us that the first step towards recovery is admitting we have a problem. This applies to our self-awareness issues as well. In Romans 7, Paul models the pathway to self-awareness by admitting he has a problem. He makes a strikingly honest confession: "I don't understand myself. Why do I struggle to do the things I want to do and keep doing the things I don't want to do?" (Romans 7:15, my translation). This might be one of the most relatable passages in Scripture.

Several of our contemporary expressions describe the internal disconnect Paul is referring to. We might say someone is "at odds with themselves," or say, "Sorry, I wasn't myself last night when I said that." It's a peculiar notion to suggest we were not ourselves, but we've all been there. We know what that feels like.

What's so powerful about Paul's confession is that he's owning this internal disconnect in his life. He's admitting he doesn't understand himself. This is the ground from which authenticity and self-awareness grows. To accept that you don't fully understand yourself.

## AUTHENTIC SELF

Your authentic self is the union of your conscious "self" and the image of God within you. In psychological terms, it's the integration of your ego and your essential self. In biblical language, your authentic self is who you are "in Christ."

The goal of this book is to unpack these concepts and shed light on the complex process of becoming your authentic self—in bite-sized chunks, on a practical level. Practicality is important. The teachings of Jesus and the New Testament point to a practical way of life. How to forgive, extend compassion, find peace, share generously, love your enemies, develop resilience, practice nonjudgment, and experience joy when things don't go our way, to name a few. Yet these Christ-like attitudes, qualities, and behaviors are the result of a profound inner

## 20  Get a Hold of Yourself

transformation, where we experience and become grounded in our authentic self. In other words, the only way to consistently and sustainably follow the practical teachings and example of Jesus is to first identify as your authentic self—in Christ.

A transformed life is the result of a transformed sense of self because our behavior is informed by our identity. You become what and who you believe you are. We sometimes refer to this as the Pygmalion effect or self-fulfilling prophecy. For instance, if a child believes they're stupid, ugly, or useless, they'll continue to find evidence that validates this belief. This is called confirmation bias. When this belief becomes embedded in the child's psyche, it shapes their self-perception. They'll begin to adopt behaviors, postures, and attitudes that reinforce this belief. This is why many of us develop self-sabotaging patterns in our lives. If I think I'm stupid, for example, I'll procrastinate or refuse to ask for help to prepare for a big exam, because a stupid person wouldn't be able to ace the test anyway.

Unfortunately, this means smart people live as if they're not; beautiful people live as if they're not; and gifted people live as if they're not. We do this because of our propensity to fulfill our embedded self-beliefs, which are typically rooted in what others have told us when we're young, vulnerable, and impressionable. We struggle to challenge these self-beliefs, even as adults, unless something or someone comes along and helps us develop new beliefs about ourselves.

When I became a homeowner in my late twenties, I didn't even consider doing renovations or fixing things around the house, because I believed I wasn't a handy guy. In my early thirties I tried to hire a friend to redo our front porch. He asked, "Why don't you do it?" I explained, "I'm not a handy guy. I can't do stuff like that." He said, "Sure you can. I'll show you how."

For the next few weeks, we reconstructed my front porch, together. At first, I was very nervous and doubted myself. But midway through the project, my limiting self-belief changed. My friend helped me see and believe I could do it. I could be handy. Since then, with the help of YouTube videos, I tackle most of our renovations and repairs around the house on my own. My transformation into a relatively handy guy began with someone helping me change my self-belief and sense of identity.

## THE CONFOUNDING TEACHING STYLE OF JESUS

Our authentic self is like a hidden reality that must be uncovered. This requires taking a brave adventure, journeying underneath the surface of our assumptions and beliefs about who we are. This adventure thrusts us into confusing and unexplored territory at first.

In Exodus, we read that the Hebrews had to wander through the wilderness before they got to the Promised Land. Similarly, the path you must travel to become your authentic self will take you through some wilderness terrain as well. A surprising aspect of the way of Jesus is that it doesn't begin with clarity, but with confusion and disorientation. Jesus leads us into the wilderness of paradox to initiate us in the upside-down kingdom of God, where we learn to receive by giving, to gain by letting go, to find victory in surrender, and to grow through subtraction.

Many of Jesus' teachings don't seem to make sense, but some of us have become so familiar with them, we no longer notice how cryptic and perplexing they are. Overexposure has left us immune to his bizarre and disconcerting instructions to "take up our cross and die daily" and "lose ourselves to find ourselves." Through familiarization and rationalization, we've dulled the provocative and paradoxical substance of Jesus' teachings, to our detriment.

We tend to miss the meaning of Jesus' more straightforward teachings as well. Have you ever wondered why Christians are widely regarded as some of the most judgmental people on earth, when Jesus' teachings on nonjudgment couldn't be more direct? "Do not judge!" (Matthew 7:1a). Clearly, we struggle to understand Jesus' message.

Most of the people in Jesus' time and culture were confused as well by his perplexing parables and pithy paradoxical sayings. Even his own disciples rarely understood what he was saying. On one occasion they challenged him, asking, "Why do you teach using confusing stories that nobody understands?" (Matthew 13:10, my paraphrase). Jesus responds, "This is why I speak . . . in parables: 'Though seeing, they do not see; though hearing, they do not hear or understand'" (Matthew 13:13).

Jesus makes it clear he was confusing people on purpose, because he wasn't trying to replace their old ideas with new ideas; he was inviting them into a completely new way of seeing and thinking. His perplexing stories and paradoxical sayings were intended to shake people from their dogmatic slumber, their default mental programming, and to awaken them to a new reality.

He revisited this idea when he said that people needed "new wineskins" to be able to receive the "new wine" of his teachings:

> No one pours new wine into old wineskins. Otherwise, the new wine will burst the skins; the wine will run out and the wineskins will be ruined. No, new wine must be poured into new wineskins. And no one after drinking

old wine wants the new, for they say, "The old is better." (Luke 5:37–39)

Just like new wine bursts old wineskins, Jesus' new insights will explode our worldview and patterns of thinking. Until we develop new wineskins, we won't like the taste of Jesus' new wine. We'll keep preferring that which reinforces our status quo and affirms our existing ideas, telling us we should keep living the way we're living. Tasting the new reality Jesus is inviting us into requires developing a whole new palate.

On several occasions Jesus uses the language of death and rebirth to describe this process. To receive new wineskins requires a form of death experience that enables us to be "reborn" and have our spiritual senses awakened. Priest and author Anthony de Mello alludes to this when he says that when a person is reborn they see all is well, but most people never see this, because they're spiritually asleep.[3] Social theorist and author bell hooks adds to this, reminding us we're prone to falling back asleep, even after we've awakened.[4]

Jesus' teachings are intended to awaken us to an entirely different reality he calls the kingdom of God. What I call the Divine Reality. Jesus wants to stir us from our superficial assumptions about God, life, ourselves, and others, exposing them for the illusions and half-truths they are, so we can see the Divine Reality, the Really Real, that is hidden in plain sight. This is why Jesus uses paradox. It shakes us, wakes us, and reveals what is hidden.

## A HIDDEN TRUTH REVEALED

As adolescents, my brother Scott and I would scour the house every December, looking for our Christmas presents. Every year we found them. And each following year, my

## 24 Get a Hold of Yourself

father would level up his hiding strategy. One year he hid them inside the paneling wall of the furnace room in our basement. Not only did we find them, when we discovered the crown jewel at the top of our Christmas wish list, a video game called *Keystone Kapers*, we decided to taste the forbidden fruit of our labor. We carefully opened the shrinkwrap packaging with a razor blade and gingerly took the cartridge out of its box. My brother and I took turns playing *Keystone Kapers* for about an hour, relishing the sweet taste of victory. Then we put it back in its box, using a thin layer of clear glue to reseal the plastic packaging and returned it to its hiding place, along with the rest of the Yuletide booty we'd discovered.

As we unwrapped our presents on Christmas morning, we feigned surprise, shouting and singing our parent's praises. The whole family gathered around the TV as I excitedly inserted our new gift into our gaming console. When the home screen of *Keystone Kapers* appeared, the top five high scores flashed across the screen, with our names displayed in bold letters beside each one. I'll never forget the look of confusion on our parents' faces as they attempted to process the discombobulating situation before them.

This scenario was, in a sense, a paradox. My parents were bewildered by a perplexing tension created by two contradictory facts:

They watched me and my brother open the video game, take it out of its sealed packaging, and put it in the gaming console.

Our names and respective high scores had already been saved in the video game memory.

My parents couldn't figure out how to reconcile these two observations because both facts couldn't be true. Or could they? As impossible as it seemed, they were. More than that, a hidden truth was eventually revealed. A truth my brother and I had hoped would remain hidden.

This is the power of paradox. It reveals hidden truths.

## WHAT IS A PARADOX?

Have you ever looked at a "Magic Eye" image? The technical term for them is *autostereogram*, which is a 3D image hidden within a 2D image. Magic Eye images typically look like an assortment of bizarre lines, shapes, and markings on the surface, but they contain a hidden 3D image if you can refocus your eyes to see it. The first time I encountered one, it took me a long time to see the 3D image. As I struggled, the person who showed it to me kept insisting, "You need to look past the surface. You need to look through it." This made no sense to me, until it happened. Where in one moment all I could see were chaotic squiggly lines, in the next my vision shifted, and a crude 3D image of a ship revealed itself.

Like a Magic Eye image, a paradox forces us to adjust and refocus our vision. It invites us to look deeper, to look through the confusing contradictions at the surface. When we do, a hidden meaning or deeper truth appears, seemingly out of nowhere. But it takes time. A paradox requires us to remain in the tension it creates, to let the hidden truth slowly unfold.

The word *paradox* comes from the Greek word *paradoxos*. It's a combination of the ancient Greek words *para*, meaning "beyond, next to, against, or contrary to," and *dokeo*, meaning "think, suppose, expect, seem, or be of opinion." When you put these two Greek words together, you get *paradox*, which means, "beyond or contrary to what you think, suppose, or expect."

What makes a paradox fruitful or meaningful is that it initiates deeper thinking and contemplation. It forces us to ponder outside or against what seems to be true, right, normal, or common sense, on the surface. A meaningful paradox is an enlightening juxtaposition. It's apocalyptic. Today, we associate the word *apocalypse* with the end of the world, but that's not what it originally meant. It comes from the Greek word *apokalypsis*, which means "to uncover, lay bare, disclose, or pull the lid off something." This is what a meaningful paradox does. It uncovers something hidden.

## THE UNIVERSE IS FILLED WITH PARADOX

Mathematical biologist J. B. S. Haldane wrote, "The universe is not only stranger than we think, it is stranger than we *can* think."[5] Haldane suggests we cannot fully understand reality with the tools of reason and scientific inquiry alone, because the universe may ultimately be an incomprehensible mystery. We can't fully understand or explain why anything exists. Numerous philosophers have suggested the greatest question is, "Why is there something rather than nothing?" No philosopher or scientist can answer this question adequately from a scientific, logical, or materialistic perspective. The only natural explanations for the existence of our universe are 1) something came from nothing, which is inconceivable, or 2) something has always existed, in some form, which is equally absurd. From a materialistic logical perspective, both options defy reason and our current understanding of reality.

Astrophysicist Neil DeGrasse Tyson puts it another way: "The universe is under no obligation to make sense to you."[6] Just because something doesn't make sense doesn't mean it isn't true. In fact, a great deal of truth doesn't make sense. For instance, light, the very "thing" we depend on to see, test, and measure everything else in the universe, is a puzzling paradox.

Light defies reason by behaving like both a particle and a wave. This is called the wave-particle duality.

The universe is full of contradictions and mysteries that defy categorization and comprehension. This led the brilliant psychoanalyst Carl Jung to write, "Only the paradox comes anywhere near comprehending the fullness of life."[7] In another essay, he wrote, "The paradox . . . reflects a higher level of intellect and, by not forcibly representing the unknowable as known, gives a more faithful picture of the real state of affairs."[8] Only paradox can help us appreciate reality as it is—full of confounding contradictions—because paradox alone has the capacity to contain these contradictions.

Let's bring this down to a personal level. *Life is short. The day is long.* Both ideas ring true to our experience, even though they appear to be saying opposite things. With the lens of paradox, we don't have to choose between them. We're enabled to see and appreciate the truth in both statements, as irreconcilable as they seem on the surface. We can accept that life is short, from a certain existential perspective, while recognizing that a lifetime is the longest amount of time any of us will ever experience. While life can feel short, a day or even an hour, when doing a job we loathe, can feel like an eternity. Paradox helps us see beyond our either/or dualistic thinking. It helps us see we don't always have to choose between two opposites to realize the truth about something, or about life in general.

## THE GOD PARADOX

Not only is the universe full of paradox, so is the Christian faith. The foundational paradox of Christianity is that God is three in one. This is called the doctrine of the Trinity, which is based on two contradictory propositions:

## 28   Get a Hold of Yourself

God is one. There is only one God and God is one being.

God is three distinct persons: God the Parent, God the Son, and God the Spirit.

On the surface, these two tenets of Christianity are contradictory. However, when held together, they reveal deeper insight into the nature of God. I've heard many analogies used to explain the paradoxical idea of the Trinity, like the three parts of an egg or the three states of water. As helpful as these analogies can be, they fail to explain the mystery of the Trinity satisfactorily. However, we begin to be transformed—to wake up and shed our old wineskins—when we realize this is the point.

The paradoxical reality of God as three in one is not to be understood as much as it's intended to open us up to new ways of thinking about and relating to God. When Christians point to a man named Jesus and say, "That human being is the infinite, omnipotent, omnipresent, omniscient Creator of the universe," it's an absurd proclamation. Yet this startling declaration is Christianity's central point: the paradoxical point. It opens our eyes to see and experience God in new and unexpected ways.

## THE ABUNDANCE OF PARADOX IN CHRIST AND CHRISTIANITY

When we look at God revealed in the person of Jesus, we are confronted with paradox after paradox. Almost everything about Jesus was paradoxical. Jesus is described in the Bible as fully divine and fully human; the Beginning (Alpha) and the End (Omega); the victim and the victor; the sacrificial lamb who was slaughtered by an empire, and the conquering Lion of Judah who has overcome the world; the judge of all, who came not to condemn (John 3:17).

**Paradox** 29

These examples are merely the tip of the iceberg, but they highlight the central theme of paradox regarding Jesus' identity in Scripture.

Paradox was also central to his teachings. A few examples:

The first will be last, and the last will be first. (Matthew 20:16)

The kingdom of God is already here, but it's also not yet here. (Luke 17:20–21)

You must lose your life, to find your life. (Matthew 10:39)

You must die, to truly live. (John 12:24)

Those who humble themselves will be exalted, and those who exalt themselves will be humbled. (Matthew 23:12)

It's more profitable to give than to receive. (Acts 20:35)

The people we see as cursed are the ones who are truly blessed. (Matthew 5:3–12)

The least will be the greatest, the greatest will be the least. (Luke 9:48)

When we are weak, we are strong. (2 Corinthians 12:10)

Such paradoxes are found throughout Scripture, especially the New Testament. Commenting on the staggering amount of paradox in the Bible, the nineteenth-century English Baptist preacher Charles Spurgeon said,

You may depend upon this fact, that paradoxes are not strange things in Scripture, but are rather the rule than the exception. Very often, those things which appear to contradict each other are only two sides of the same truth, and he who would get at the truth itself must look at them both, and follow them both.[9]

Spurgeon highlights one of the keys to unleashing the revelatory power of paradox: we must hold both sides of the paradox and live in the tension it creates, to glimpse the deeper hidden meaning contained in its contradictions. This isn't as easy as it might sound.

Many Christian denominations and sects have devised their own doctrinal particularities, with the goal (sometimes intentionally, sometimes unwittingly) of eliminating or diminishing the paradoxical nature of Christianity. They do this by overemphasizing one aspect of the message over its opposite. For example, some elevate Jesus' divinity at the expense of his humanity. Others overemphasize God's grace over God's justice, or God's sovereignty over the free will of humanity.

Our drive to resolve contradictions and force paradoxes to be rational stems from our need for things to make sense. We experience discomfort, anxiety, fear, and meaninglessness when they don't. For instance, when we encounter contradictions in our faith, or between our faith and reality, we're compelled to rationalize away the paradox. If we pray for the healing of a loved one, for example, and they aren't healed, this doesn't make sense if we believe that God cares, prayer works, and Jesus meant it when he said, "I will do whatever you ask in my name." When something like this happens, we do whatever we need to do, and believe whatever we need to believe, to make our world make sense again. We might conclude we didn't pray with enough faith or that God had a good reason for allowing this to happen, that we can't understand. Or perhaps the only way we can resolve this contradiction is to conclude the God we believed in doesn't exist.

We strive to eliminate paradoxes because it's easier to cling to a rationalized version of our faith, or reject our faith as irrational, than allow paradox to break apart our assumptions and beliefs about who God is and how God works in the world. Unfortunately, when we refuse to hold on to these contradictions, we negate the paradoxical nature of Christ's message and miss out on its transformative power to reveal deeper hidden truths.

Maintaining this paradoxical tension has always been foundational to orthodox Christianity. It was one of the litmus tests the early church used to recognize heresy. One of the earliest beliefs the church dismissed as heresy was Docetism, the belief that Christ couldn't be a real human being because Christ was God, and God cannot be human. For Docetists, Christ did not have a real human body, he only appeared to be a human. They were attempting to make Jesus' nature logical, but the early church dismissed it, because it was attempting to deny or resolve the paradoxical tension of Jesus being 100 percent God and 100 percent human.

The reason paradox was and is so important to Christianity is simple: it's embedded in nearly every aspect of Jesus and his teachings. The early church recognized that this paradoxical tension was essential to the gospel message, because it flips the script of our theology in a powerful way. Instead of us attempting to grasp Christ and his message, paradox insists we allow Christ and his message to grasp us.

## THE KINGDOM OF GOD PARADOX

The paradoxes found in Jesus' message become exciting invitations when we stop viewing them as stumbling blocks to a rational faith and see them as pathways to live in the Divine Reality (kingdom of God). Jesus describes the Divine Reality as

32   **Get a Hold of Yourself**

a paradoxical reality, full of contradictions. It's something we receive, yet it's something we must find and enter. It's already here, but it's also not yet here. It comes from the heavenly realm, yet it's within us. To see it, we must become spiritually mature, while becoming like little children.

The primary truth Jesus reveals about the Divine Reality is that *God is with us. Right here. Right now.* This contradicted the perceived reality of his original audience. They were living in occupied territory, oppressed by the Romans. It felt like God had abandoned them. On the surface, God was nowhere to be seen, but Jesus taught them God's presence is always among us—only hidden.

Most of Jesus' parables are about the kingdom of God, where he teaches us the Divine Reality is like hidden treasure that's buried in a field or inside the shell of an oyster or underneath the surface of a river, lake, or sea (Matthew 13:44–47). The paradoxical message of Jesus constantly points us to this deeper truth—that God is *with* us—but we need *eyes to see* and *ears to hear* this hidden reality.

## THE PARADOX OF YOU

Not only is God, Jesus, Christianity, and the universe full of paradox. So are you. We're all walking paradoxes. We're greedy and generous, strong and vulnerable, courageous and cowardly, honest and deceitful. Our inclination is to hide, ignore, or fix our contradictions, but they're actually gifts that can help us discover the hidden treasure beneath the surface of who we are.

When we come to understand Jesus' message fully, we see that discovering the hidden treasure of the Divine Reality is also to become aware of the mystery of our authentic self. They are connected. This is why Jesus says the Divine Reality

## Paradox 33

(the kingdom of God) is within you (Luke 17:21). Our authentic self is in part a hidden reality, the pearl inside the oyster, the treasure buried in these jars of clay.

In this book, we'll look at some of the paradoxes found in Jesus' teachings that can help us develop an awareness of the Divine Reality within us and all around us. We'll learn how to become our authentic self, not by resolving, transcending, or eliminating our contradictions, but by exploring the gaps they create and finding the hidden treasures they reveal.

We'll see that as we follow the paradoxical teachings of Jesus, we gain access to a different way of seeing, thinking, and being, which enables us to grow and live with freedom, joy, purpose, and abundance, in our paradoxical reality of being both sinners and saints, serpents and doves.

# 2

# EXPECTATIONS

In 2012 I embarked upon a pilgrimage to Scotland, the homeland of my ancestors, where I purchased the Watson family crest. I was disappointed when I first saw it, nestled among the other family crests in the shop. Most of them had bold and intimidating images of lions, swords, or falcons. The Watson crest was rather dull in comparison, bearing an image of a humble human hand, accompanied by the inscription "Confisus viribus," which means, "Trusting in my strength."

Although I was unimpressed with the uninspiring image, the motto fit our family surprisingly well. Especially my father. He epitomizes it to a degree both impressive and ridiculous, in equal measure. Growing up, I observed him routinely refuse help from well-intentioned neighbors, as if their offerings were personal attacks on his masculinity. Why would he need to borrow his neighbor's ladder to repair an eaves trough, when he could stand on a stool, balanced on top of an old chair missing one leg, that he'd found at the dump last week. Ladders were for the weak and elderly, for men with no imagination.

My father has relied on the strength of his own two hands for over seven decades now, and those hands are so calloused, he no longer has feeling in them. When he washes dishes, the water is the perfect temperature for making coffee, just shy of

36 **Get a Hold of Yourself**

a rolling boil. I once saw him take a cookie sheet out of the oven with his bare hands. Very rapidly mind you, but still. Why would he do such a thing? Our coat of arms isn't a picture of an oven mitt, is it? No. We're Watsons. We trust in the strength of our own hands.

I was surprised to learn that our clan—a social group larger than our family, with shared ancestry, history, and culture—also had a coat of arms. Our coat of arms has a picture of two hands on it, holding the branches of an odd-looking oak tree with a thick trunk. (The Watson obsession with hands is as confusing to me as it is to you.) The motto on our coat of arms is "Inspirata floruit," which translates, "Unexpectedly flourishing." This one might be even more fitting than our family crest motto, although the two complement one another quite well. I mean, would you expect a family that trusts in the strength of their own hands for combat, hunting, and farming, to survive, let alone flourish? Of course not. Nobody would.

When I first saw our coat of arms motto, I assumed it was referring to the Watson clan surpassing the low expectations of the other clans around us. I imagined them exclaiming, "You're kidding! The Watsons are still around? The family that doesn't use ladders or oven mitts. That's surprising. They're doing quite well, you say? Flourishing even? Wow. I did not expect that. Good for them."

Upon further reflection, I wondered if our motto might be referring to the expectations we place upon ourselves and one another. No one is more surprised than us when we collectively or individually flourish in some way. The Scottish Watsons are a pessimistic bunch in general. We expect disappointment. We seem drawn to it. Yet we also expect to find humor in life's ups and downs. Whether we're thriving or struggling, suffering or celebrating, dancing or arguing, we're almost always laughing.

Expectations 37

You might say we're negative, but in a jolly way. The truth is we're complicated and contradictory, like most families.

## BEYOND EXPECTATIONS

All families have expectations that often resemble a Dickens novel. We expect the best, while expecting the worst. Our families may expect us to be proud but humble, honest but keep up appearances, independent but obedient, gentle but assertive, compliant yet ambitious, generous while taking care of our own first. It can feel like our family expectations are pulling us in a thousand different directions.

As children and adolescents, we internalize the expectations others place upon us, especially our families. Even the expectations we rebel against. They impact and influence us for the rest of our lives, one way or another. Sometimes we're aware of our conflicted and contradictory expectations, but often we're not. Sometimes they stay hidden, in our subconscious, manifesting in surprising or self-sabotaging ways. Left unexamined, our expectations can wreak havoc in our lives. They have tremendous power over us. They can motivate us or demoralize us, lift us or crush us.

Sometimes we might find ourselves flourishing beyond our expectations. However, it's more common to find ourselves failing to live up to them. After all, it's tough to be physically fit, intelligent, accomplished, confident, a successful go-getter who climbs the corporate ladder, while being sensitive, nurturing, and present with our families, while maintaining an impeccable home and yard, volunteering at the local soup kitchen every weekend, and coaching our kids' Little League team.

Not only do we strive to fulfill too many expectations, many of them are unrealistic or contradictory. We might feel obligated to be the strong, stoic, silent type, while also being vulnerable, emotional, and communicative. Or to be attractive and charming, without drawing too much attention to ourselves.

Our expectations often serve as reminders that we don't measure up. That we aren't good enough, successful enough, smart enough, or disciplined enough.

The expectations we place upon others, the world, and God are just as detrimental to our well-being as the ones we place upon ourselves. Because our happiness and contentment is often dependent on the fulfillment of our expectations. When our expectations are unattainable, we're like prisoners in a cage of our own design. The good news is the key to unlock this cage and reclaim our freedom is within our grasp. It's as simple as learning to expect the unexpected.

## ARE YOU SURPRISABLE?

When my wife Tammy first heard the story about me opening my gifts before Christmas, she was as disturbed and disappointed as my parents were.

"Why would you do something like that? Why would you want to ruin the surprise?"

Tammy can't understand this part of me that must solve any puzzle, riddle, or surprise as swiftly as possible, but it's how I'm wired. What she calls "ruining" I call "figuring out." She can't understand this, because she loves surprises. She's not alone. Many people claim to love surprises. But they're mistaken. Nobody loves surprises. Not really. When people say they love surprises, what they really mean is they love any unanticipated act, event, or situation that fulfills a general expectation or desire they have. What they really mean is they love to be pleasantly surprised. Which is like saying you love eating fish, unless it tastes fishy.

Nobody loves surprises that involve tragedy, bad news, or disappointment.

*Surprise, it's cancer.*

*Surprise, your family has been in a terrible car accident.*

*Surprise, we have to let you go. Please clean out your desk immediately.*

Nobody in their right mind would delight in such surprises. Yet many of life's surprises are like this. In a word, unpleasant. Things we'd rather avoid, because they bring disappointment, not delight.

One of my favorite classic Christmas movies is *National Lampoon's Christmas Vacation*. In this film, the protagonist Clark Griswold was expecting a big year-end bonus from work, so he made an advance down payment on a swimming pool installation in his backyard. Finally, a card from his company arrived on Christmas Eve. He opened it with great anticipation. Much to his dismay, it did not contain the big bonus he was expecting. Instead, he received a Jelly of the Month Club membership.

His response to this surprise?

"If this isn't the biggest bag-over-the-head, punch-in-the-face I ever got."[1]

This is how many of life's surprises feel. Like a punch in the face. This is why we proactively, though often subconsciously, protect ourselves from life's surprises. If that fails, we may choose to resist the surprises life bestows upon us.

Most of us are guilty of ignoring, undermining, or refusing to accept surprising revelations about ourselves, our partner, child, friend, political leader, pastor, or hero, because it's too challenging or threatening to accept the information the surprise is disclosing. "My child would never do that! Our governor is a good man. This is fake news, a scandalous smear job."

Over my twenty-seven years of pastoring, I've observed many Christians refuse to acknowledge surprising revelations that contradict their theology. They choose to ignore, dismiss, or deny a shocking insight, because it challenges the status quo of their worldview. Atheists and agnostics do this as well. It's not just religious people. We're all prone to doing this because we're inclined to see what we want to see. We suffer from what psychologists call motivated perception and confirmation bias. These terms simply mean we're hardwired to see things, others, and the world in ways that validate our desires, commitments, decisions, beliefs, assumptions, and preferences, even in the face of surprising but compelling evidence to the contrary.

To be open to truth means that when surprises come along and challenge our status quo, we're open to them and respond to them appropriately. We change our beliefs, habits, and lifestyles in light of the surprising revelation. These moments are called breakthroughs for a reason, because they break through our resistance to change. However, breakthroughs are rare. For example, in 2012 a study on health behavior reported that most people diagnosed with a life-debilitating condition or illness did not adopt healthier behaviors.[2] They refused to change their lifestyles, even though these changes would mean their health would improve and they'd live longer. It's amazing how often we ignore surprising revelations, even when our health and life is on the line, to maintain the status quo of our lives.

## THE MESSIAH SURPRISE

When you read through the Gospels, it becomes clear the arrival of the Messiah named Yeshua (who most of us call Jesus today) was a surprise. He was a surprise to Mary, and

**Expectations** *41*

certainly to Joseph, but also to his contemporaries. Jesus didn't fit their expectations of who and what the Messiah would be and do. They were expecting the Messiah to fulfill certain expectations, like overthrowing their oppressors. Even the angel Gabriel seemed to expect this. When he told Mary she would become pregnant and give birth to the Messiah, he said, "He will be great and will be called the Son of the Most High. The Lord God will give him the throne of his father David, and he will reign over Jacob's descendants forever; his kingdom will never end" (Luke 1:32–33).

Here's the thing. This didn't happen. Certainly not in a way any reasonable person was expecting. Jesus didn't reestablish the throne of David, overthrow their Roman oppressors and rule over the kingdom of Israel forever. He was arrested and killed by the Romans thirty-three years after his birth.

The Magnificat is the name given to Mary's song of praise, recorded in the gospel of Luke. It's her response to the angel Gabriel's good news announcing she will give birth to the Messiah. In her song, she declares her expectations that her son, the Messiah, will "scatter the proud, bring down the powerful, and take away the abundance of the rich" (Luke 1:51–54, my paraphrase).

Again, this didn't happen. Not in Mary's lifetime. Not in anyone's lifetime. The proud, rich, and powerful still exist and continue to rule our world today.

The night Jesus was born, angels appeared to some shepherds on the hills of Judea, outside of Bethlehem. The angels said, "We bring good tidings of great joy for all people. The Messiah is born in Bethlehem. Glory to God in the highest and peace on earth!" (Luke 2:10–14, my paraphrase).

This was the most exciting thing to happen in the little town of Bethlehem for centuries, maybe its entire history.

## 42  Get a Hold of Yourself

The next big event in Bethlehem happened about a year and half later. The slaughter of the innocents. King Herod sent soldiers to Bethlehem and the surrounding area, to murder all the male children under the age of two. The arrival of the Messiah certainly didn't bring great joy to those families. The Messiah's birth didn't bring peace to this region of the earth. This unspeakable massacre was the worst kind of surprise. It was the opposite of what Bethlehem was expecting after receiving the good news the angels had announced to the shepherds. Yet this part of the Christmas story illustrates a very important truth:

*Life is full of surprises—and many of life's surprises bring disappointment, hardship, and pain. And having faith in God doesn't change this. Jesus doesn't change this.*

This is a hard truth. It comes as a surprise to many people of faith. That being a good person, serving God, believing in Jesus and following his teachings—none of this spares us from the disappointment, hardship, and suffering of life. Because that's not what faith does.

## THE SURPRISING LETDOWN OF FAITH

Many Christians expect God to protect them and their loved ones from the unwanted surprises of life. They expect their faith to spare them from disappointment. But the story of Jesus reminds us this isn't the case.

I'm not saying miracles never happen. They do, sometimes. I believe God responds to our prayers, and intervenes on our behalf, on occasion. However, these miraculous moments are the exception, not the rule. Usually when we ask God for a miracle, it doesn't happen, at least not the way we were expecting and hoping for.

Jesus says just a small amount of faith can move mountains, and it's true. But this doesn't mean faith is a magic wand. Faith doesn't guarantee all our expectations and desires will be fulfilled, and, our worst nightmares won't happen. It doesn't work like that. Faith is about who and what we trust.

An important faith question to ask yourself is: Do I trust God? Or am I putting my trust in the fulfillment of my expectations? Do I trust God's Spirit to lead me to peace, joy, and fulfillment, or am I trusting my expected outcomes to bring me peace, joy, and fulfillment? The difference may seem subtle but it's huge.

Most Christians throughout history, across all cultures, have had moments of deep disappointment. Where it felt like God and their faith didn't come through for them. Some of us walk away from our faith, because it doesn't live up to our expectations. However, billions of Christians throughout history have also discovered, when life gets hard, painful, and disappointing, when they can't understand what's happening or not happening, this is when they need God and their faith the most. One reason for this is because the paradoxical dynamic of faith does something very powerful. It liberates us from the tyranny of our expectations.

## THE PARADOXICAL POWER OF FAITH

One of the definitions of paradox is "beyond or contrary to expectations." The paradoxical dynamic of faith helps us stop expecting our expectations to lead us to fulfillment, and trust God to fulfill us. It enables us to find a deeper source of peace, joy, and meaning that isn't dependent on having our expectations fulfilled. It enables us to find contentment, no matter what happens.

## 44 Get a Hold of Yourself

This is not to undermine the deep pain we experience when tragedy befalls us or our loved ones, or when people leave, betray, or abuse us. This suffering is very real. God sees our suffering and cares. In Jesus, we meet a God who became one of us, suffered like us, walks with us in our suffering, and wants to bring healing to our pain. When we suffer loss, abuse, betrayal, or injustice, our faith helps us know and feel that God cares.

Healthy faith helps us grieve and respond in appropriate ways. However, when the time is right, faith also calls us to challenge our expectations. When something unfair, painful, or even tragic happens, our tendency is to assume this isn't how life should be, or at least not how *our lives* should be. This way of thinking is normal, but it's also unrealistic. If we have any grasp of history, we know life is full of suffering, injustice, and tragedy. It always has been.

At some point, we'll need to ask ourselves why we expect life not to be hard, painful, and disappointing. What do we base this expectation on? Why do we assume it's our job, or God's job, or other people's jobs, to make reality fulfill our expectations? Why do we trust the "rightness" of our expectations more than the "rightness" of reality? Why are we convinced we know how reality ought to unfold?

These are very hard questions. These are the kinds of questions the book of Job presents us with in the Bible, that Job himself was confronted with, after suffering in ways most of us can't imagine. I'm not suggesting we need answers to these questions. I'm merely encouraging us to spend time with them. To be curious about our expectations and the role they have in our lives.

In *Man's Search for Meaning*, Viktor Frankl recounts his experience of losing everything, including his wife, father, mother, and brother, in Nazi concentration camps. The last thing he possessed in Auschwitz, that gave him a sense of purpose and hope, was his manuscript he secretly worked on and kept hidden. The guards eventually found it and destroyed it.

As he was about to give in to despair, he had an epiphany. He realized no matter what they did to him, and took from him, they couldn't take his freedom to choose how to respond. He could still choose to be grateful and hopeful. So that's what he did. He found little things to help him find joy and appreciate beauty.

Frankl realized he could not change his situation, but he could change his perspective and himself. He said he stopped asking questions of life and focused on answering the question life was asking him. He realized life is asking *us* what the meaning of life is and concluded that when we live responsibly, honorably, we become the answer. We become the meaning. And when our suffering finds meaning, he proposed that it is no longer suffering. It's a sacrifice for something bigger, life's grand unfolding, that we can't always understand, but we can trust. He said this was consistently exemplified in the concentration camps by the people who trusted in God.

As recounted in the book of Acts, in Philippi, Paul and Silas were arrested and imprisoned without a fair trial. They were beaten, tortured, and thrown into a dirty dungeon, bound by chains, potentially for the rest of their lives. That night, they responded to their situation by singing joyful songs of praise and thanksgiving to God (Acts 16:22–25). Their faith in God provided them with something more powerful than the fulfillment of their expectations; it gave them access to genuine peace, joy, and gratitude, regardless of whether their expectations about what was fair or right were fulfilled or not.

## 46 Get a Hold of Yourself

I'm aware these are deeply challenging ideas, but they're true. When our mental and emotional states are no longer dependent on the fulfillment of our expectations, we're liberated to find peace, joy, and hope, no matter what's happening. We open the door to the cage of our expectations, free to find happiness and contentment in the unexpected.

## THE PRACTICE OF CURIOSITY

To expect the unexpected replaces our need for certainty—with the gift of curiosity. Our attachment to certainty expects joy and contentment to come from reality meeting or exceeding our expectations. Which won't happen. Not all the time. Not even most of the time. Genuine and sustainable fulfillment comes only when our curiosity exceeds our expectations.

Genuine faith makes us curious. It makes us surprisable. Curiosity is the drive to dig deeper and be open to new ways of seeing, thinking, and understanding. It's the capacity to be intrigued with the layers contained in everything, big and small, joyful and sad, surprising and mundane, ordinary and extraordinary. It's what motivates us to explore the things that puzzle us, as well as the things that seem obvious, commonplace, or inconsequential. Curiosity helps us see that everyone and everything has deeper layers of mystery and meaning, if we have "eyes to see and ears to hear." The stronger our curiosity grows, the more interesting life becomes. All aspects of life.

In our default mode, what matters most is having our expectations fulfilled. This is how we think we'll find happiness. Yet this only sets us up for disappointment. Some of us have experienced this disappointment in devastating ways.

When we're expecting our best friend to be true and they stab us in the back. When we're expecting to grow old with the

**Expectations** 47

love of our life and they walk out on us. When we're expecting to outlive our children and one of them is taken from us.

As painful as life can be, at some point we can only surrender and accept reality for what it is. Or as some mystics say, sometimes we must forgive reality for being the way it is. Life is hard, painful, and often unfair. Expecting or insisting it be otherwise will only increase our disappointment and suffering. Accepting the disappointment, pain, and sorrow of our unmet expectations is step one. Being open to finding peace, joy, and fulfillment in unexpected ways is step two.

This doesn't mean we won't grieve, weep, feel anger and despair. We will. But curiosity can offer us a way to move forward, to eventually get past the haunting ghosts of our unmet expectations and open up to new ways—unexpected ways—to find peace, joy, and fulfillment.

It's not that expectations are wrong. Expectations and anticipation can play a vital role in our lives. One of the keys to well-being is having something to look forward to. A key to happiness and fulfillment is making progress, which requires planning, setting goals, and having expectations. However, we must be able to pivot when reality doesn't meet our expectations. Which will happen. When it does, we can stay stuck in the disappointment and despair of reality not meeting our expectations. Or we can be curious.

It's not always easy to accept what has happened, to accept life is the way it is, but we can at least be curious. We can be curious if there might be unexpected ways God can help us find meaning, peace, and even joy again.

I don't know why God lets painful and tragic things happen to us. But one of the things that has sustained me through my darkest nights has been curiosity. Being curious if there's some truth to the claim God's grace is sufficient

48  **Get a Hold of Yourself**

(see 2 Corinthians 12:9). To be curious if there's a possibility "God is causing everything to work together for good" (see Romans 8:28 NLT).

I realize Bible passages like these can be applied in ways that amplify our suffering and pain. Yet they also give us something to be curious about. What if they're true? What if God can take what happens to us, including what others intended for harm, and make something good from it?

Every time I've been heartbroken—when I lost people I loved, when I felt rejected for being me, when people betrayed and abandoned me—I grieved. We must grieve. But it was curiosity that eventually helped me move forward, every time. I wondered if there was more to life. I became curious if there was more hope, peace, and contentment available to me than I was currently experiencing. I wondered if I'd find my passion and enthusiasm for life again, in ways I didn't expect. I wondered if I would be surprised by joy again.

I'm not suggesting you dive into the deep end and start practicing curiosity with your most painful experiences. I would suggest the opposite. Start by being curious when your expectations are met. Ask yourself questions like: "Why did things work out this time? Why did that make me happy? Why did it only make me happy for a few hours or days? Did I feel more excitement and joy in the anticipation leading up to this moment or in the actual fulfillment of my expectation?" There is a lot to be curious about when things go according to our plans.

As we consistently practice curiosity, it becomes an automatic response, like muscle memory. Even when things don't turn out the way we want or expect, we increasingly respond with curiosity. We ask questions like, "Why didn't that work out? Why did that make me feel sad? What is my

**Expectations**  49

disappointment rooted in? What is my reaction to this revealing to me, or about me?"

When our expectations are unmet, we can always be curious, and our curiosity can redirect us to find fulfillment in other ways. I don't mean the event or unmet expectation itself will become fulfilling. But as we go through the experience, curiosity can offer us a path to find fulfillment in finding a deeper level of meaning in our lives. This may not help us understand why certain things happened, or why life is the way it is. But it can help us understand why we are the way we are, why we're reacting and feeling the way we are, and how to move forward.

A popular quote that's not stated but suggested in the journal reflections of nineteenth-century philosopher Soren Kierkegaard says, "Life can only be understood backwards; but it must be lived forwards." Only in hindsight are we able to find meaning in many of life's events. In seminary, I was encouraged to start journaling as a spiritual practice. It has been a gift to be able to look back on what I was experiencing in certain moments and see them with new eyes, years or even decades later. It's amazing how much insight and perspective time offers.

One friend recently introduced me to keeping a loss and disappointment journal. I've found it to be an excellent way to practice curiosity in hindsight. Here are the three steps.

1. Write down your loss or disappointment and the date it happened.
2. A month later revisit it and ask, "What did I learn through this?"
3. Six months or a year later, revisit it and ask, "What is something good that came out of this?"

*50*   **Get a Hold of Yourself**

As we engage curiosity as a life practice, we begin to expect the unexpected. We expect to find insight in unexpected places and people. We expect to find growth, excitement, peace, and even joy in unexpected ways, circumstances, and experiences. Even amid hardship, adversity, and pain.

## EXPECT AN UNEXPECTED REWARD

Jesus, and the Bible in general, consistently challenge us to expect the unexpected with God. Here's a specific example. In the gospel of Luke, Jesus teaches us to give to others, especially those who can't repay us, without expecting anything in return. When we do this, our reward will be great (Luke 6:30–35a). Jesus is presenting us with yet another paradox. If you don't expect a reward, you can expect a reward.

Jesus is challenging us to be curious about our motivations in life. He's teaching us to live, love, and give, without expecting anything in return. When we do, ironically, we can expect God to reward us. One way of interpreting this is, when we do the right thing because it's the right thing to do, when we act with love and generosity because it's a genuine expression of our authentic self, our reward from God will be great. We'll experience a higher quality of life. The highest quality of life possible, in fact. A life filled with love, joy, peace, and contentment. But it's paradoxical. We can only expect this great reward if we're not expecting a reward.

I was driving to work one cold and rainy November morning when I saw a young man in a T-shirt, at a bus stop, shivering in the frigid fall weather. I remembered I had an extra jacket in my trunk and a scripture passage sprang to mind: "Let the man who has two coats give one to the man who has none" (see Luke 3:11). Without thinking about it, I pulled

**Expectations** *51*

over, grabbed my extra coat, ran over to the young man and gave him the jacket. As I turned to leave, I said, "God told me to give this to you. Have a great day."

I ran back to my car and jumped in, to get out of the pouring rain. Before driving off, I looked in the rearview mirror. When I saw the comical look of bewilderment on the young man's face, mixed with relief from the stinging wind and rain as he put the jacket on, it filled my heart with so much joy, I couldn't contain it. I erupted into a ridiculous fit of laughter, interposed with spontaneous songs of praise to God. I would've appeared completely unhinged if anyone had been in the car with me. My delight and laughter continued my entire drive to work. It was the most exuberant commute I've ever experienced. This state of bliss stayed with me the rest of the day.

In fact, I woke up the next morning and jumped out of bed, enthusiastically looking forward to what opportunities I might encounter that day, to join God at work in the world. My normal run-of-the-mill routine became an exciting adventure, as I opened myself up to God interrupting the slog of the mundane, with unexpected opportunities to join the Spirit in making the world a better place, one act of love and obedience at a time.

I'm not expecting any kind of accolades for my experiment in following Jesus. It was an old jacket. It wasn't much of a sacrifice. My point is that giving away my jacket, for free, with no expectation of anything in return, brought me a far greater reward than if I'd sold it for twenty dollars or exchanged it for something in return. I now understood Jesus' paradoxical wisdom about receiving a greater reward from God, by giving without expecting anything in return. Because I'd experienced it.

## EXPECTATIONS AND IDENTITY

What does this have to do with our authentic self? The journey of becoming one's authentic self requires a capacity to expect the unexpected, with regards to who we are. Arguably the greatest influence on our sense of identity is the expectations other people, groups, and society place upon us, which we internalize. A major step in the quest to become our authentic self is learning to practice curiosity—with regard to ourselves. As we release our assumptions about who we are, and relax our expectations on who we need to be, we free ourselves to expect the unexpected in ourselves. We realize we're a mystery that is slowly unfolding, in God's time.

As we learn to expect the unexpected, we stop resisting when life takes us down unexpected roads. And we're enabled to receive the surprising hidden truths these roads reveal to us, about us. This is what the next few chapters are about.

3

# DESIRE

My friend's wealthy and hospitable parents heard I loved beef, so they took us to an upscale eatery that claimed to have the best steak in the city. As a poor university student from modest means, I was completely out of my element. Why were there three forks set before me? And why did our server have an assistant?

I was shocked when I opened the menu. One item cost more than my monthly rent at the time. I tactfully ordered the cheapest steak on the menu. Top sirloin, well done. Before I finished though, the father interrupted me,

"He'll have the ribeye, medium rare."

I assumed he was having a bit of fun with me, so I laughed and turned to the server to repeat my original order. Once again, he cut me off: "Trust me, Troy, this is the best steak in town. You'll love it. He'll have the ribeye, medium rare."

The server nodded and collected our menus.

My initial state of confusion quickly transitioned into disgust, as I anticipated cutting into a half-cooked piece of steak. The thought of putting medium rare beef into my mouth made me nauseous. I grew up in a modest and simple home, where we cooked our meat just shy of burnt crisp. Chewing

## Get a Hold of Yourself

overcooked, dried out, inexpensive cuts of meat often caused mild pain and discomfort in our jaws, but that's how we knew it was safe for human consumption. It hurt to eat it. We had a system.

We had no conviction everyone should eat like us. Well done steak is an acquired taste, I suppose. It might not be for everyone, but neither was medium rare. This is what bothered me. The nerve of my friend's father, insisting I eat his steak, his way, betraying the tradition of my heritage. He'd crossed a line. I thought about confronting him but relented. He was generously paying for my meal, and I was his guest.

When I saw our server coming with our meals, my annoyance gave way to anxiety. The pressure mounted as my meal was placed in front of me. All eyes were upon me, waiting for me to take a bite of the "best steak in town." Even the server stuck around to watch.

As I looked down at the abundance of utensils in front of me, I found myself on the precipice of a full-blown panic attack. Not only was I overwhelmed with the possibility of vomiting the moment I inserted a piece of medium rare beef into my mouth, I was now worried I would have done so using the wrong fork. My breath quickened; my heart raced. I was approaching a breaking point.

For a moment, I considered standing up and running out of the restaurant. I'd have to start a new life with new friends. This chapter of my life would be over. Clearly. I could never talk to this friend again, or anyone we both knew. Yet this path of starting over seemed easier than eating a medium rare ribeye.

Unfortunately, the server was standing right beside me, blocking my escape route, as if sensing I was a flight risk. There was no way out. So I inhaled, gave myself a quick pep talk and surrendered to my fate. I cut off a bite and stifled my gag reflex as the red juices flowed onto the plate. I closed my eyes and brought the piece to my lips. As I began to chew, an intense primal pleasure of delectable perfection exploded in my mouth. The meat was so tender and succulent. The texture and taste mingled in utopian symmetry. A perfect balance of savory, buttery, peppery, and marbled meaty decadence danced upon my tongue. I couldn't believe the flavors.

I experienced a culinary paradigm shift of celestial proportions that evening. It was like I was eating steak for the first time. In a sense, I was. This moment changed my life. From that day forward, my favorite food on planet Earth was and is a finely aged medium rare ribeye. A half-cooked hunk of meat. The very thing I'd regarded as deeply disturbing and utterly disgusting my entire life. Until I tasted it.

## YOU DON'T KNOW WHAT YOU WANT

In 2004, best-selling author Malcolm Gladwell gave a TED Talk presentation focusing on Howard Moskowitz's spaghetti sauce research in the 1980s.[1] Moskowitz was an American market researcher and psychophysicist, hired by Prego to help them come up with a better spaghetti sauce to compete against their rival Ragu. In his test groups, Moskowitz found roughly a third of the people were looking for a plain sauce, a third preferred a spicy sauce, and a third favored a chunky sauce. What made this discovery so significant, and lucrative for Prego, was that there was no chunky spaghetti sauce on the market at the time.

Yet the most interesting revelation from Moskowitz's research was that the people who preferred the chunky spaghetti sauce didn't know this when the testing began. Not one person said they were looking for a chunky spaghetti sauce at

## 56 Get a Hold of Yourself

the beginning of the test trials. It was only after they tasted it, that they said this was the kind of spaghetti sauce they preferred. Moskowitz's research had uncovered a universal truth: people often don't know what they want, until they taste or experience it.

This is what happened to me with the medium rare ribeye. It's happened to me many times since then. I didn't know I loved shawarma, pad thai, chicken tikka masala, or spicy pierogi pizza, until I tried them. I didn't know I loved jazz music until I heard Miles Davis. I wasn't aware I needed meditation in my life, till I tried it and kept at it. I'm sure you can think of a few examples of this in your own life.

## MY FIRST TASTE OF THE SPIRIT

One of my earliest memories of church was at a midweek children's event. I was seven years old and unfamiliar with church or Christianity at the time. Church was a new thing for our family. My parents' marriage was on the rocks, and they were desperate, looking for anything to save them and their relationship. It worked. They're still together, forty-five years later.

The church had brought in a special guest speaker that night, for the kids. After the puppet show, he asked us to bow our heads, close our eyes and invite Jesus into our hearts. It felt weird. It wasn't just the oddness of the speaker's hushed voice and the soft organ music now playing in the background. What made it especially peculiar for me was the resistance I felt. I wasn't indifferent or bored. I felt a struggle within me.

I opened my eyes and looked around at the other kids. Most of them were sitting peacefully, with their eyes closed. A few of the rowdier boys were joking around, elbowing each other and giggling. They weren't struggling with this. Why

**Desire** 57

was I? I peered around the sleepy old church building and my eyes fell upon the cross at the front of the sanctuary. After a brief pause, I prayed. I still can't remember why. That's still a mystery to me. I didn't feel pressured or obligated. Maybe I was curious? I can't recall. Whatever the reason, I began to talk to God. Then something unexpected happened.

I felt a sudden intensity of desire for God. I remember this vividly. Something shifted, like I'd tuned in to a deeper longing. I remember a part of my brain thinking it was strange how sincere my desire for God had become. Then something else happened. I became aware of a presence. My Creator was with me. Divine Presence surrounded me. God's presence felt tangible and dense, yet so gentle and beautiful. A field of pure light and peace embraced me, saturating my entire being. It was overwhelming. It was also deeply personal. I felt completely understood and loved in that moment. Like my Creator was hugging me and saying, "Troy, you are my beloved son. I take great pleasure in you, for who you are." I felt full, free, whole. My entire body was buzzing. Every cell in my body was enlivened, from head to toe. It felt like time stood still. Like I was experiencing eternity.

I'm not sure how long this heightened state lasted, but it changed me. Permanently. There was no going back. This moment was so powerful, so real, so beautiful; I knew this was what I wanted. God was what I wanted. More than anything. And I knew Jesus, the one I'd prayed to, had made this happen, or was involved somehow. I didn't understand what had happened or how it worked. That didn't matter. I'd been awakened to something bigger than me. Something real, amazing, divine.

I still struggle to find the right words to describe what happened. As a seven-year-old, I had even fewer words to

*58* **Get a Hold of Yourself**

describe it. But it was so exciting, I wanted to talk about it. I asked some of the other kids if they'd prayed. A few of them said yes. I asked if they'd experienced anything. They all responded the same way. "Not really. What do you mean?" When I tried to put my experience into words, they looked at me as if I'd grown antlers. No one had a clue what I was talking about. This confused me. It also taught me to keep my spiritual experiences to myself. Later in life, I realized people can't understand these transcendent God encounters until they've experienced one for themselves.

The result of this experience was profound. I knew God was real and was what I wanted in my life, more than anything. I didn't know that when I walked into that little rural church that summer evening, forty-five years ago, but I walked out being more certain of it than anything.

## DO WHAT YOU WANT

Several years ago, my spiritual director asked me, "What do *you* want, Troy? What is it you really want?"

It struck me as a ridiculous question. I told her as much. But her question stayed with me. I sensed the Holy Spirit echoing this question during my prayer times over the next few days. Then the next few weeks. Finally, I decided to contemplate it. "What do you want, Troy?" To my surprise, I didn't have a clear answer.

Growing up as a fundamentalist Christian, the question "What do you want?" didn't matter. Who cares what I want. What I want is probably sinful. The only question that mattered was, "What does God want?" That's the question I've been asking the Creator most of my life.

Asking what God wants is an important prayer. An essential prayer. I've prayed it often, and I've grown much because of it. Jesus himself lived this prayer. He said, "For I have come . . . not to do my will but to do the will of him who sent me" (John 6:38). In the garden of Gethsemane he prayed, "Not my will, but yours be done" (Luke 22:42). Like Jesus, we should seek God's will in prayer.

Yet it shouldn't be our only prayer. The Scriptures also teach us to "bring our requests to God" (Philippians 4:6) because the Most High cares about what we want. A number of scripture passages tell us God wants to give us the desires of our heart. Such as Psalm 37:4: "Take delight in the LORD, and he will give you the desires of your heart." (See also John 15:7; Matthew 21:22; Philippians 4:19; Jeremiah 29:11.)

If this is true, and it is, it's probably important to know what the desires of our hearts are.

One of the underlying calls of the way of Jesus is to align the desires of our hearts with the desires of the Most High (see 1 John 5:14). How can we know if our desires are aligned with God's desires? Studying the Bible is a good place to start. Scripture says the Creator desires love, forgiveness, generosity, mercy, compassion, justice, and peace, to name a few. Around twenty-seven hundred years ago, the prophet Micah offered a succinct list, writing, "What does the Lord require of you? To act justly and to love mercy and to walk humbly with your God" (Micah 6:8).

What God wants is obvious. And when your desires align with God's desires, you can rest assured, God wants to give you the desires of your heart.

## THE DESIRES OF OUR HEART

It changes your life when you believe the Creator wants to give you the desires of your heart. That God is in your corner and wants you to be happy and fulfilled. However, we must first figure out what it is we want. What we *really, really* want. This is a tougher question to answer than you might think. Right now, for instance, I want poutine, a bagel, and a chocolate croissant. (I'm currently in an area of Quebec that specializes in such delicacies.) Yet I also want to lose a few pounds and get more fit. That's the dilemma of desire. We want it all. We often want things that are contradictory to other things we want. So, we must discern what it is we *really, really* want. Not just what we sort of want.

Underneath our contradictory desires, there's often a deeper hidden desire that's not obvious on the surface. For instance, you might want to spend more time at work to advance your career or business, but you also want to spend more time with your partner, children, loved ones, or friends. You might want to take on a side hustle or purchase a rental property to increase your cash flow, but you also want to simplify your life. As a parent, you want to enroll your child in every potential program and club available, ensuring they have every opportunity to excel, but you also want to spend more quality time at home together, as a family.

Discerning the hidden desire of what we truly want takes time. Here's an exercise that has been helpful for me. I call it "Uncovering Our Core Desires."

### Step 1: Write out what you want.
Let's say I answer, *"I want more money."*

### Step 2: Write out what it is you think your answer in step 1 will give you.
What exactly do I think more money will give me?
*More money would give me relief from the stress of being in debt and the burden of struggling to pay bills. It would*

*give me the freedom to do what I want: to travel, see amazing places, eat great food, do fun things, have nice things, and not worry about finances. It would enable me to be generous to family, friends, and those less fortunate than myself.*

**Step 3: Write out what you think the things you named in step 2 will give you.**

If I reflect on the things I wrote down in step 2, I'll eventually start to see what it is I'm really looking for.

In step 2, I wrote, "Relief from financial stress and worry."

What is it I'm really looking for here?

*Peace of mind.*

I wrote, "The ability to do what I want."

What do I think this will give me?

*Freedom. Personal power.*

I wrote, "The ability to travel, see amazing places, eat great food, have nice things, do fun things."

What do I think these will give me?

*New experiences, pleasure, adventure, access to beauty.*

"The ability to be generous to others." This speaks for itself.

**Step 4: Is what you answered in step 1 the only way, or even the best way, to get what you wrote down in step 3?**

If what I'm really looking for is *peace of mind, freedom, personal power, adventure, new experiences, pleasure, beauty,* and *the capacity to be generous,* is more money the way to attain this? Does the Creator offer another way to find these things? Does the way of Jesus offer a better way to attain the things I *really, really want?*

It's important to uncover our deepest desires and name what it is we want in life. Only with clarity and focus can we wholeheartedly invite the Spirit to help us fulfill the desires of our heart. When we do this, we often discover the truth of what the Sufi mystic Rumi said: "It's rigged—everything, in your favor."[2]

Countless people throughout history have found that when we are in tune with our true desires, and in harmony with God's desires (which are aimed at the greater good of all—not just us as individuals) the Spirit will guide and assist us in fulfilling our heart's desires. In a way that brings goodness to others, as well as ourselves. I've found this to be true in my own life. However, I've also discovered the fulfillment of our true desires will probably happen in ways we didn't anticipate. Remember, with God we must "expect the unexpected."

## MORE IS NOT ENOUGH

Several years ago, one of my wealthiest friends met with me, asking me to pray for him. He lamented, "I've got everything I could ever want, Troy, but I'm still not happy."

I've walked with enough wealthy people to know money can't satisfy the deepest desires of our hearts. Although there's substantial evidence a certain amount of money increases our happiness and quality of life, there's even more evidence that the happiest and most fulfilled people in the world are not wealthy. They often have below average incomes. If you've traveled to developing countries, for instance, you've probably met plenty of people with less money and possessions than you have, who are happier and more fulfilled than you are. This has certainly been my experience. While it's true a certain amount of money is essential to survive and be happy, wealth is not. Wealth is often a hindrance to genuine happiness. Because more stuff, including more money, is just more to worry about.

In an episode of the television show *The Simpsons*, the protagonist Homer has a conversation with Mr. Burns, his boss. He comments that Mr. Burns is the richest guy he knows, to which Mr. Burns responds, "Ah yes. But I'd trade it all—*for a little more.*"[3]

With things like money, it's never enough. It doesn't matter how much we have; we always want more. Because when we're pursuing things like money, we're chasing after things we've been programmed to want. Things our world has convinced us will make us happy. Not what we truly want. The problem is most of us don't know what we really want. So we keep chasing more of what we've been conditioned to want, hoping it will someday, somehow, be enough.

Until we discover and name what we really want in life, we'll keep looking for more of what we've been programmed to think will bring us happiness and fulfillment. But as we accumulate more of the same, we find our satisfaction fades as quickly as it comes.

## THE HEDONIC TREADMILL

Psychologists refer to the tendency of people to consistently return to their default level of happiness, regardless of what happens to them, as the hedonic treadmill. Our happiness levels tend to rise temporarily with positive experiences and events but quickly return to our baseline level. This is why the boost of happiness we experience when we get a new job, car, house, or relationship is short-lived. Before we know it, we're feeling the same discontentment and desire as before, looking forward to the next new thing or event to bring us another boost.

Consider all the things and experiences you were convinced, at one point in your life, would make you happy and content. When you finally got them, did they make you happy and content? Permanently? No. You eventually jumped back on the hedonic treadmill of life.

There's another theory called Parkinson's Second Law. It proposes our expenses always increase in proportion to our income growth, because our expectations and desires rise in tandem. Our lifestyles typically rise in proportion to our cash flow. Our financial baseline, or what we believe we need to live, increases to match our income. What this means is "enough" is never enough.

Many of us are tirelessly running on the hedonic treadmill, the hamster wheel of life, perpetually seeking more, wondering when "enough" will finally be enough. The problem is that we're expecting the accumulation of what we've been programmed to want to somehow satisfy our heart's true desires. Hoping more of what we want on the surface will eventually fulfill the deepest desires of our inner being. This doesn't work. It can't work.

## MANY DARK CAVES CONTAIN DRAGONS AND GOLD

There's a popular saying, attributed to Joseph Campbell: "The cave you fear to enter holds the treasure you seek."[4] What he's saying is the things you really want in life are often found in the places you least want to go. The path to the things we desire most, like freedom, peace, joy, healing, and love, usually take us down roads we'd rather not travel. They lead us to scary caves, as Campbell suggests.

Have you ever wondered why many people who have survived a life-threatening diagnosis or gone through a near-death experience find a deeper level of peace, contentment, and purpose in their lives? Few of us would seek a near-death experience, or a serious battle with cancer, or attempt to do something nobody believes we can do, yet these are the kinds of scary caves Campbell is referring to. The ones that contain the true treasure of life we're all looking for.

Consider the gospel message of Jesus. It's essentially this: The greatest treasure in life (God's presence, salvation, healing, redemption) is found by picking up your cross and dying to yourself. The path of Christ leads to death. And there's no cave more frightening than death.

Consider the last message the risen Jesus gives to Peter in John 21:18. Here's my paraphrase: "When you were younger and less mature, you went wherever you wanted to go, Peter. However, as you grow and mature, someone else will lead you where you don't want to go." This is the paradoxical path Jesus invites us all to follow. A path where we find what we're looking for, by being led to places we don't want to go.

## GOD FULFILLS OUR TRUE DESIRES IN UNEXPECTED WAYS

You're probably familiar with the saying, "God moves in mysterious ways." Well God often *moves us* in mysterious ways as well. Ways that don't always make sense to us. There are many reasons for this, but one is revealed in Moskowitz's maxim. Because we don't know what we want until we experience it. Like my friend's father, who ordered the medium rare ribeye for me nearly thirty years ago, our Creator often pushes us into situations or circumstances we'd rather avoid, or onto paths we'd rather not travel, because the Most High knows it's only through that experience or on that path we'll discover what it is we truly desire.

I'm not saying every painful, difficult, and uncomfortable thing that happens to you is God leading you to scary caves.

## 66 Get a Hold of Yourself

Not at all. Much of what happens in life is and will remain a mystery. I'm also not claiming that you'll exit every scary cave grateful for the experience. I can recall many experiences of being pressured into eating things that turned out to be disgusting, not a delightful surprise. The only thing I was grateful for was when the meal was over. Not every cloud has a silver lining. I'm not saying we'll always find something positive in every difficult or painful experience.

What I'm saying is this: God will meet us in the scary caves life sometimes leads us to and will help us discover hidden treasure in those caves. Sometimes that treasure is simply an awareness of God's presence with us. To sense God walking with us, through the scary cave. To know we're not alone.

As priceless as this treasure is, we often discover more than this. We might discover we're stronger than we think. Or we find clarity on what really matters in life, or access a deeper level of resilience, endurance, and confidence. Or we might discover we're capable of so much more than we ever thought possible.

Sometimes when it feels like life or the universe is taking us in the wrong direction or pushing us into places or experiences that make us uncomfortable or afraid, it turns out to be good news. Sometimes it's an act of providence and mercy, moving us towards discovering what it is we truly want in life. We often resist these movements of disguised grace. We resist entering the caves we fear to tread. Yet it's only as we open ourselves to the leading of the Spirit, and embrace the paradoxical way of Jesus, that we begin to open ourselves to the possibility of finding treasure in the places we least expect.

This paradox is confounding. Frightening even. But it's true. The treasure we're seeking in life, such as peace of mind, freedom, healing, inner strength, or a new start, is often found in the situation we'd prefer to avoid, the difficult conversation we want to ignore, the conflict we'd rather circumvent, or the inner wound or memory we'd rather repress. Discovering the treasure of one's authentic self will not happen at the surface. It requires entering the caverns and crevices that lead us deeper into the depths of who we are. Like Peter, this will require an openness and willingness to be led to places we don't want to go.

# 4

# DEATH

When I was twelve years old, two sixteen-year-old boys in our small church community died the same year. Luke was diagnosed with cancer and died a few months later. Kent was found in a barn with a rope around his neck. These tragic deaths devastated our church community. Kent's suicide was particularly shocking and confusing. He was a popular, intelligent, and creative young man, who seemed to have everything going for him. Everyone loved him, or so it seemed. It didn't make sense. It felt like there was a curse on our church. I began to wonder if any of us young people would make it past sixteen.

Years later I came across a quote from Maya Angelou. "Few, if any, survive their teens. Most surrender to the vague but murderous pressure of adult conformity. It becomes easier to die and avoid conflict than to maintain a constant battle with the superior forces of maturity."[1] Most of the teenagers in my childhood church made it into adulthood, but not with our authentic self intact. I think we all suffered the kind of death Angelou refers to. The death of conformity.

I've discovered there are different kinds of deaths we can experience in life, not just physical death. In fact, Jesus talks about a particularly strange kind of death in his teachings. A death he says is beneficial. Necessary.

## DEATH IS THE WAY TO LIFE

Perhaps the most disturbing of Jesus' paradoxical teachings is that death is the gateway to life. To truly live, we must die before we die. He talks about this a lot. He says, "Whoever wants to be my disciple must deny themselves and bear their own cross and follow me" (Matthew 16:24; Luke 9:23; Luke 14:27). He says, "If you cling to your life, you will lose it; but if you give up your life for me, you will find it" (see Matthew 10:39; 16:25; Mark 8:35; Luke 9:24). In the gospel of John he says, "Truly, I tell you, unless a kernel of wheat falls to the ground and dies, it remains only a seed. But if it dies, it bears much fruit" (see John 12:24–25).

Paul also talks about this. He writes, "I have been crucified with Christ and I no longer live . . ." (Galatians 2:20). He encourages us to "present our bodies as a living sacrifice" (Romans 12:1) and tells those of us who have faith in Christ, "You have died, and your life is hidden with Christ in God" (Colossians 3:3).

What kind of death are Jesus and Paul talking about? They're obviously not talking about a literal physical death. So what are they referring to?

Death is ultimately the loss of your "self" as you are. Aging prepares us for this incrementally. Helping us see life is one big loss project, losing one thing after another. As we age, we lose our luscious hair, smooth skin, youthful beauty, and vitality. We experience hearing loss, muscle loss, decreased bone density, energy loss, and cognitive decline. We eventually lose our independence, our driver's license, our capacity to live on our own. We lose friends and loved ones. Finally, we lose our lives.

In death, the self you know and have known ceases to exist. In the afterlife, what and who you are is ultimately unknown. Religious people have beliefs regarding what happens to our immortal souls after we die, but we really don't know what our bodies, personalities, relationships, and abilities will be in the next life. It's all speculative. Will we walk around with our youthful smiles, smooth skin, and luscious hair in heaven? We don't know.

What we do know is that we'll die. We don't have a choice in the matter. At some point we'll be forced to let go of everything we are and have been. The death to self Jesus talks about, however, is a choice. It's willingly letting your sense of "self" cease to exist, before your physical death forces you to. It's letting go of the person you've known yourself to be. This means letting go of all your ideas, beliefs, and assumptions about who you are and who you've been.

Most of us have had small deaths in our lives. When we lose an important aspect of our identities. Some people experience such profound loss we can only describe it as cruel. I think of Andrew, who attended the first church I pastored. Andrew was a talented athlete on a sports scholarship at university. He suffered a tragic car accident that left him physically and mentally impaired, no longer able to play sports or continue his studies at university. He was no longer the same person he was. Yet Andrew is one of the most joyful and content people I've ever met. The peace and joy that shines through him whenever he walks into the room is inspiring.

Most of us would say what happened to Andrew is tragic, but that's not how he would describe it. Yes, he had to grieve tremendous loss, but he's found something most of us are still looking for. Peace, joy, and contentment. I think the reason we struggle to accept such loss as anything but tragic is because we think things like academic, athletic, and career success are what will bring us happiness. Yet Andrew has found a deeper level of happiness than 99 percent of the people I've met, without those things. After losing those things, when they were right in his grasp.

I believe the death to self Jesus points us to is ultimately letting go of our belief that anything besides living in the Divine Reality, as our authentic self, will bring us true and sustainable peace, joy, and contentment.

Most of us won't undergo a life-changing loss like Andrew that completely changes who we are. In a sense, our death to self will be more difficult for us to accept, because life won't forcefully take away our old sense of self. We'll have to willingly surrender it. We'll have to let go of who we've known ourselves to be, to be born anew. For that's what death to self is about. Being reborn. As our authentic self.

Jesus doesn't invite us to die for the purpose of dying. He invites us to die so we can truly live. To live a life filled with peace, joy, love, and freedom. Paul puts it this way, "We become a new creation. The old has passed away. Behold, the new has come!" (See 2 Corinthians 5:17). There's something on the other side of this death to self that's completely liberating.

But we can't just jump to the rebirth part. We must die to self first. This isn't easy. We resist death. We fear it. This is normal. So we usually have to reframe our relationship with death first, before we can willingly experience death to self.

## DEATH IS NOT THE PROBLEM

Christians believe Jesus has claimed victory over death. Jesus' resurrection shows us death doesn't have the final word, for Jesus has conquered the grave. We celebrate this as good news, because it is. One of the most important things we learn from Jesus about death is that it's not the end.

Yet we can only understand and experience this by walking through the valley of the shadow of death, with God, and realize we have nothing to fear. We must face death, letting go of who we are, trusting in Christ's resurrection power, to know and experience that death is not the end. Only then can we see that it leads to resurrection and new life.

We must let Jesus conquer the fear of death in us, breaking the illusion that death is permanent. However, we still must die. All of us. Jesus doesn't spare us from death. In fact, he saves us through death. Not only his death, but our own. This is why he teaches us we must bear our own cross, not just believe in the saving power of his cross. As important and redemptive as his death is, Jesus says we must bear our own cross and die to our own "self," to be spiritually awakened and live in the Divine Reality.

There's so much to unpack with regard to what this means, which I will do in later chapters, but it's important to notice the underlying point of Jesus' teaching here. *Death is not the problem. It's part of the solution.*

There's a lot to process in this provocative statement. Death is an essential part of the path moving us towards the treasure we're seeking. For starters, Jesus is teaching us that our fear of death, our resistance to death, hinders us from truly living. So we must reframe our relationship with death. Instead of fearing it, resisting it, and labeling it as purely bad, we must be open to receiving the wisdom and gifts death offers us.

## THIS MAGIC MOMENT

In my thirties, I met a Buddhist monk who talked about treating everyone and everything as if they're already gone. When we do this, we experience each moment as a gift that's almost magical, transcending time.

"Imagine the person you're holding has already passed," he said. "Yet, here in this moment, this glorious moment, you're blessed with the opportunity to enjoy their company one last time. When we live this way, we treat each person, each thing, each moment, the way they deserve to be treated. As a precious gift."

After twenty-seven years of pastoring, one of the most common things I hear grieving people say is, "I wish I could hold them one more time. I wish I could see their smile and tell them I love them one more time." This Buddhist monk was saying we need to live as if we're getting that opportunity now, in every moment, with the people in our lives. This might sound weird or melodramatic, but the truth is we don't know how much time we have left with anyone or anything. In the grand scheme of things, the ones we love are as good as gone. James says, "What is your life? You are a mist that appears for a little while and then vanishes" (James 4:14). Tomorrow is never guaranteed, for any of us.

The brilliance of this monk's teaching, however, was in his suggestion to treat each moment not as the last moment, but as if it's *after* the last moment. To live as if the people and things you love and appreciate are already gone. Yet now—in this magic moment—you've been gifted with one last chance to enjoy them. Blessed with the very thing you'll long for more than anything else in the not-so-distant future. One more moment to hold them and tell them you love them.

Buddhist monks call this meditative practice *maraṇasati*, which means "Remember death." The Stoic philosophers also had a practice of reflecting on death. They called it *memento mori*, which means "Remember that you must die." Most cultures, in most eras, have been keener to reflect on death than modern Western cultures. They understood death has much to teach us, and the longer we delay learning from death, the more superficial and fear-based our lives become.

**Death** *75*

In 2010 I visited a strange place in Rome called the Crypt of the Capuchins. The Capuchins were monks who separated from the Franciscans in 1525. They wanted to return to the true spirit of Saint Francis and live out more authentically his emphasis on simplicity and poverty. Their crypt in the middle of Rome now houses the remains of about thirty-six hundred Capuchin brothers. It's not a fancy or elaborate place. Quite the opposite. It's a narrow, musty, and moderately lit underground tunnel, located beneath the church of Santa Maria della Concezione dei Cappuccini. It consists of five small, plain rooms, each one decorated with bones, skulls, and a few complete skeletons: the remains of the Capuchin brothers who died there over the centuries.

Over the opening to the last chapel, there's an inscription that says, "What you are now, we once were. What we are now, you will become."

I visited another Chapel of Bones in Evora, Portugal. Upon one wall of the chapel was a poem that read,

> Where are you going in such a hurry, traveler?
> Pause . . . do not advance your travel.
> You have no greater concern, than this one:
> That on which you focus your sight.
> Recall how many have passed from this world,
> Reflect on your similar end.
> There is good reason to do so;
> If only all did the same.
> Ponder, you so influenced by fate,
> Among the many concerns of the world,
> So little do you reflect on death.
> If by chance you glance at this place,
> Stop . . . for the sake of your journey,

## 76   Get a Hold of Yourself

The longer you pause,
the further on your journey you will be.[2]

As I stood reading this poem, surrounded by bones, I was struck by the paradox, "The longer you pause [and reflect on your death], the further on your journey you will be." In our spiritual journeys, we advance by slowing down, not by hurrying up. How much of our hurried, distracted lives in the twenty-first century is about avoiding thinking about the inevitable reality called death?

My son recently showed me a video clip of a social media influencer asking someone how they would feel if he gave them ten million dollars. The person said they would be ecstatic. Nothing could take away their excitement and joy. It would be the greatest gift they ever received. Then the influencer said, "But there's one condition. If I give you the money, you won't wake up tomorrow morning. Do you still want it?" They said, "Of course not."

As contrived as this social media stunt was, it helps us see that death puts everything into perspective. We see that we value waking up every morning more than ten million dollars. It makes us question why we don't wake up every morning with the same excitement and joy that a gift of ten million dollars would bring us. Death helps us see how precious life is. It makes life meaningful. It helps us see the true value of each sunrise and sunset. Remembering death reminds us how blessed we are to be alive. That the gift of today, with all its inconveniences, struggles, and hardship, is more valuable than all the money in the world.

I try to tune in to the school of death at least once a month. I contemplate my death, not to entertain some sick twisted fantasy, but to let the clarity of death's voice illuminate what

**Death** 77

really matters in life. The Roman emperor and Stoic philosopher Marcus Aurelius wrote in his private journal, "You could leave life right now. Let that determine what you do and say and think."[3] The Greek philosopher Socrates said, "Those who pursue philosophy aright, study nothing but dying and being dead."[4] A bold statement, uttered by arguably the most famous philosopher to ever live.

As I contemplate my death, it awakens me from my tendency to numb out, coast on autopilot, complain, waste energy, and let minor things bother me. I imagine an angel visiting me, telling me I have three days left to live. What would I do with the time I have left? I wouldn't sweat the small stuff, that's for sure. I wouldn't waste time fretting over being overcharged at the grocery store or getting even with the colleague who made a snarky comment about me. I would invest my time, focus, and energy on the people and things that matter. The things that last. The things that will survive death's fire. The Bible says the only things that will remain forever are, "faith, hope, and love. But the greatest of these is love" (1 Corinthians 13:13).

I've discovered nothing has more respect for love than death. I can't think of anything that nurtures love within me, more than death. When I imagine the people I love passing away, I feel a wave of sadness, but I also experience a tremendous surge of love for them. I feel so much love, it changes how I see and interact with them. My annoyance over my son leaving the bathroom light on, again, or my wife not putting the car keys where they belong, again, or my friend not returning my text quickly enough, again, totally fades. I feel nothing but love and appreciation for them. I cherish who they are and thank God for the gift of them being in my life. All judgment, frustration, resentment, and disappointment disappear. I feel only love and gratitude in my heart.

I always hug my wife and children after my monthly death contemplation. I'm tempted to hug complete strangers. (I usually don't.) I'm always more kind, compassionate, encouraging and gentler with others. For a while at least. That's why I need to do it monthly.

Try it yourself. Consider the death of someone you love. Picture them. See their face. Now picture losing them. Is there anything that makes you feel greater love for that person than this? Is there anything that makes you more grateful for the time you have with them? To reflect on death is to honestly reflect on life, and see that love is everything.

## THE BAPTISM OF DEATH

Many Christians refer to water baptism as a form of death. I was raised Baptist and that's how we viewed it. That's why we dunked people. Full immersion, baby. I realize some of you might have been sprinkled, and that's fine. The Mennonite denomination I'm part of embraces all forms of water baptism; sprinkling, pouring, or immersion. Water baptism is just a symbol of a deeper reality. Having said that, I'm partial to the symbolism of immersion as it fits how the apostle Paul describes baptism in the book of Romans. He says when we're lowered into the water, it's like being buried with Jesus. When we come back up out of the water, it's like we are resurrected with Jesus.

When I was baptized at the age of twelve, my childhood pastor read Romans 6:2–8, then he said, "Baptism is like entering a watery grave. Underneath the water, we say goodbye to our old lives. As we resurface, we're starting a new life in Christ." Then he plunged me underneath the water of our baptismal. As I came up out of the water, everyone cheered and clapped. My parents were beaming with pride and joy. It was a special celebration, pregnant with meaning for me still.

Yet a few days after my baptism I wondered, "Is that it?" Although I felt like I'd solidified my commitment to follow Jesus and had a deeper sense of belonging in my church community, I didn't really feel different. I didn't feel like a new creature. Deep down, I knew there had to be more to this death and rebirth experience Jesus talked about.

Water baptism is only a symbol of our death and rebirth experience. An important symbol that points to something else. That's what symbols do. My baptism was a symbol of another experience to come: the baptism of the Holy Spirit. (See Acts 19:1–6.) More on that later. It also gave me an image to make sense of the paradoxical reality of our end being a new beginning. A reminder that when we die to self and let go of our sense of who we are, we rise as a new creature. Like a phoenix out of the ashes. Like a butterfly from the cocoon. Yet the rising comes after the descending. New life comes after death to self.

## IN THE END IS OUR BEGINNING

One of the wisest and most gracious human beings I've ever met is a one-hundred-year-old woman named Reta. Reta was a founding member of the church where I currently minister. She passed away while I was working on the final draft of this book. My last conversation with Reta was about her favorite hymn, "In the bulb there is a flower." This song explains that for the flower contained within the bulb to live, the bulb must die. It must bravely let go of itself and split apart. It must cease to be a bulb for the flower within it to sprout and grow.

This hymn is based on Jesus' teachings in the gospel of John, where he essentially says,

Unless a kernel of wheat falls to the ground and dies, it remains only a single seed. But if it dies, it produces many seeds. Anyone who clings to their life will lose it, while anyone who lets go of their life in this world will find life is eternal. (John 12:24–25, my translation)

The death to self we experience becomes a new birth, a spiritual beginning. We discover the tomb is also a womb. We see our authentic self is a beautiful flower within us. But our default mindset is to identify with being the bulb. Unless we're willing to stop clinging to our identity as the bulb, we'll never be able to let the flower of our authentic self sprout and flourish. This requires the death of the bulb. The death of the bulb isn't ultimately about death though, it's about life. Letting the flower within us grow and thrive. Death to self is only destructive to the bulb. Not the flower. The death to self we experience doesn't hurt us, not who we really are, it only dismantles who we think we are.

This is why Jesus says we must lose ourselves to find ourselves. That is what the next chapter is about.

5

# IDENTITY

During my sophomore year in university, Ashley and I were walking down a busy roadway, when someone began shouting lewd remarks at Ashley, from a car parked on the shoulder of the road opposite us. The driver then leaned out of his window and dared me to come over and confront them. So I did. I waited for a break in traffic and swaggered over like a tough guy, with as much bravado as I could muster.

When I reached their car, three muscular men in their mid-twenties got out and surrounded me. The driver was pointing a 38-caliber snub nose pistol at my chest. I no longer felt like a tough guy. I felt like a frightened chicken, wondering, "Why did I cross to the other side of the road?"

Fortunately, this happened in the middle of the afternoon, on a busy road with many witnesses. This probably saved my life. I survived the incident relatively unscathed, but something had shifted in me. This close encounter with death initiated a profound introspective journey of personal deconstruction, culminating with an unsettling realization that I'd tried to be a tough guy, because I didn't really know who I was.

## DECONSTRUCTING IDENTITY

One of the most important life principles on our quest to live a meaningful life is: "Know thyself and to thine own self be true." These are the words of two very wise individuals. The saying "Know thyself" is attributed to Socrates, and it was Shakespeare who wrote, "To thine own self be true."[1] Put them together, and this wisdom nugget really packs a punch.

Before you can be true to yourself, you must know yourself. And knowing who you really are is no small task. According to Jesus, "You must lose your 'self' to find your self." (See Matthew 10:39; 16:25; Mark 8:35; Luke 9:24; John 12:25.)

Personal development typically involves trying on different identities to see how they fit. Adolescents often experiment with new styles and personas when they move to a new town, school, or university. Some young adults backpack through Europe or South America to "find themselves." Others immerse themselves online to craft or recraft their personal brand. Some folks make surprising changes in their forties and fifties that others label a mid-life crisis. We all experiment with our identities and reinvent ourselves at some point, as we attempt to find or create an identity that's true to who we are, or that's in line with how we want to be perceived.

Constantly reinventing ourselves can be symptomatic of deeper issues, but for the most part, exploring and experimenting with one's identity is a natural and healthy aspect of personal development. A more common hindrance to becoming our authentic self is reinforcing a particular identity for too long. When we fixate on an identity we settled on years or decades ago, even though it might have been truthful and useful to us at the time, it can stunt our growth in the present. Like the proverbial middle-aged man who's living in the past, constantly rehashing the glory days of being an all-star football player in high school. Like Uncle Rico in the film *Napoleon Dynamite*. There usually comes a point when the identities we solidified in an earlier life stage no longer fit.

For a season it might have been helpful, even healthy, to perceive ourselves as a bulb. But we must let that identity die to grow and thrive as the flower within. It often takes a crisis or some kind of rock-bottom experience for us to let go of an identity we've held onto for a while. And the longer we've held onto it, the more it usually takes for us to let go of it.

## EMBRACING VULNERABILITY

After my frightening encounter, I realized I'd crossed that road for reasons other than confronting the defamers of Ashley's good name. I did it to prove I was a real man. To Ashley, yes, but more importantly to myself. Somewhere along life's road I'd been convinced I needed to be a tough guy to be a real man. Real men were tough guys. If I wasn't a tough guy, I wasn't a real man.

This began a deconstruction process for me regarding masculinity and identity. I discovered I'd accepted a male archetype that was not true, at least not comprehensively true, and then began exploring other models of masculinity besides the "tough guy" model I'd subconsciously accepted as an adolescent. In our current time and culture, we're deconstructing gender. That's another topic altogether. My point here is, in 1994, I discovered I didn't need to be a tough guy to be a real man.

Up to this point in my life, I'd resisted being vulnerable. Real men didn't show vulnerability. Vulnerability was weakness. After this event, I saw vulnerability was a window into reality. It wasn't something to be resisted, eliminated, or ashamed of—it was a truth to accept. It doesn't matter how tough or strong we are, we're all vulnerable. It doesn't matter how much you can bench press or deadlift, if someone pulls out a gun and shoots you in the face, it's game over. We're all vulnerable.

This was a liberating "aha" moment for me. My vulnerability was important for me to acknowledge and accept, because it was the truth. We're all vulnerable in this world, whether we admit it or not. Accepting this is essential in our pursuit of becoming our authentic self, because the closer we live in harmony with truth, the more freedom and authenticity we experience. As Jesus said, the truth will set you free (John 8:32). You can't be free if you're not living in truth. And the truth is, we're vulnerable.

## THE NECESSITY AND DANGERS OF DECONSTRUCTION

There are periods of personal deconstruction we must undergo to allow the truth to set us free. Deconstruction is ultimately the breaking down, dismantling, and analyzing of systems, ideas, assumptions, and language to find the truth buried underneath them. To grow, we'll need to deconstruct our understanding of who we are, who we've been conditioned and cultured to be, and who we're convinced we need to be. This process is necessary to know ourselves and be true to ourselves. Yet we must also be cautious, for the deconstruction process can become an addiction that enslaves us. It can turn into a process with no end, like a child asking the question "Why?" indefinitely.

There's always another layer of the onion to peel, if we're looking for it. Eventually this leads us nowhere constructive. When we become fixated on breaking things down, without seeking the truth that resides underneath what we're dismantling, that's destruction, not deconstruction. When the goal is

**Identity** 85

to relentlessly tear down or tear apart what exists, rather than find something to rebuild on, it's unhelpful, unproductive, and meaningless. The ultimate purpose of deconstruction is to gain understanding, so we can rebuild or construct something new or better.

In our personal growth journeys, the end goal isn't perpetual deconstruction, it's constructing a life that's in line with the truth of who we are, as far as we're capable of understanding it. We'll never arrive at absolute truth and complete self-awareness. However, we can make progress in these pursuits. This requires us to act, living as if the truth we've rediscovered is true, to discern if it is true. Truth cannot be merely analyzed theoretically, it must be embodied and lived to be tested and proved. All the while we must remain open to further deconstruction, when we notice something isn't adding up in our worldview or with how we identify ourselves.

There are several reasons we become addicted to deconstruction. The main reason is it's easier than construction. It only takes a few hours to burn down a building that took many months or even years to construct. To bring it to a personal level, if we feel insecure or inferior around certain people, it's easier to criticize and tear them down, in attempts to eliminate the perception (or our projection) of their superiority, than deal with the root issues of our own insecurity and feelings of inferiority. It's easier to mock someone who tries yet struggles to answer a complicated question the teacher asks, and point out what's wrong with their answer, than it is to raise our hand and risk answering the question ourselves. It's easier to condemn a start-up company that fails to develop adequately equitable hiring policies, and boycott them, or vandalize their warehouse to make a statement, than it is to start our own company with more equitable hiring policies.

Many of us are drawn to deconstruction because we're overwhelmed with everything that's wrong in our lives, cities, institutions, and world. It feels important and virtuous to point out everything that's wrong. Because things need to change. Yet things will only change if we follow up our deconstruction with action that is constructive and creative. If we only tear down what exists, and don't rebuild anything in its place, the things we've torn down will simply be rebuilt by the constructive people, powers, and institutions who built them in the first place.

It's hard work to make something. This includes making something of ourselves. This is why we can get stuck in deconstructing ourselves. We become our own worst critics, for many reasons. One reason is because it's easier to beat ourselves up and tear ourselves down than it is to put in the hard work to grow, change, heal, and build a meaningful life.

## THE NARROW PATH OF GROWTH

Jesus talks about his path being narrow (Matthew 7:13–14). His narrow path leads us to losing ourselves to find our authentic self. This narrow path has a ditch on either side of it. Sometimes we run into obstacles on the narrow path that force us to detour into one of these ditches. Sometimes it's the only way to move forward. The key is to not get stuck in these ditches.

On one side is the ditch of deconstruction. I've already described how we get stuck in this ditch. On the other side is the ditch of status quo reinforcement. This is our propensity to defend and reinforce our beliefs, values, identities, institutions, and systems of power, as they are. We ignore what's wrong, unjust, dysfunctional, and untrue to maintain the status quo, usually because it benefits us somehow.

Author and life coach Tony Robbins says, "The strongest force in the human personality is the need to stay consistent with how we define ourselves."[2] Most of us are prone to getting stuck in the ditch of reinforcing the status quo of our identities, far more than the ditch of deconstruction. We spend most of our adult lives here. We seem hardwired to do whatever it takes to maintain our current worldview and self-concept.

## THE TRUTH WILL SET YOU FREE, BUT FIRST...

The Hebrews were held captive in Egypt for four hundred years. Finally, God led them on a journey towards freedom in Canaan. Unfortunately, the journey was tedious and took longer than expected. Eventually they started yearning for the good old days as slaves back in Egypt.

The Hebrews' journey to Canaan is symbolic of our journey. On our quest to find freedom, we often reach a point of preferring the enslavement of our old identities, instead of wandering in the unknown. We prefer to go back to Egypt, to slavery, even though we were unhappy and unfulfilled there. We go back to our abusive ex or find someone just like him, rather than be alone. We start drinking again, even though it almost destroyed our career and our relationships. We go back to the dead-end job we hate, because we couldn't get the loan to start our own business.

We return to slavery in Egypt because the grass always seems greener on the other side of the fence, no matter which side we're on. This is especially true when we're wandering in the desert. We prefer our old life of mediocrity, or even misery, because the discomfort, hardship, and pain we feel in our present wilderness eclipses the discomfort, hardship, and pain we experienced back in Egypt, which has dimmed in our memories over time. In addition, we don't know how things

## 88   Get a Hold of Yourself

are going to work out in the unknown desert. At least back in Egypt we knew what to expect. Better the devil you know than the devil you don't.

There's another reason we return to, or avoid leaving, the familiar. We're afraid we might run into the truth in the unknown wilderness. Why would we be afraid of the truth? In the words of some activists, "The truth will set you free, but first it will tick you off."

Sometimes new people, places, and contexts can reveal inconvenient and uncomfortable truths about us, which we've become blind to. Like we've all grown accustomed to the smell of our own homes and can no longer detect it. Yet when we visit a new place, we pick up on its scent immediately. And when new people visit our homes, they detect our home's scent right away.

Strangers can often see things in us that people close to us have either become blind to or have learned to ignore and avoid so they don't push our buttons. When the people we know do push our buttons, we usually assume that reveals something negative about them, not us. It's easier to dismiss our pesky brother-in-law, for example, when he says we talk too much, because he's always been overly critical of us. But when the new staff member in accounting, who seems likable and reasonable to everyone, says we talk too much, it gets our attention.

We've all got buttons, and they'll inevitably get pushed. We've all been in situations where someone says something to us, or about us, that triggers us or makes us snap. Later, when we calm down, if we're relatively healthy, we'll acknowledge we overreacted. If we're growing in self-awareness, we'll be able to see that many of our overreactions occur because what the other person said contained truth. When you overreact and get disproportionately offended, annoyed, or hurt by

Identity  89

what others say, practice curiosity after you've settled down. There's often a truth nugget, buried in that mountain of reactivity, that can help set you free.

This doesn't mean the other person wasn't being rude, disrespectful, or even malicious when they said it. It doesn't mean you don't need to establish boundaries with them in the future or stand up to them if it's appropriate and worth the bother. It simply means there might have been truth in their statement.

The truth isn't always easy to swallow and digest. Especially truth about ourselves. It seems humorous to me now, but it was initially difficult for me to accept I wasn't cut out for life as a tough guy. Because I assumed that meant I wasn't a real man. Accepting the truth and letting go of the illusions, assumptions, and false beliefs we have about ourselves is hard and painful, especially the first few times we do it. Once we go through this a few times and see we've come through the other side stronger, wiser, and more at peace, we learn to trust the process. We know it's working for good, in our favor, over the long run.

Over time, we're not threatened when we sense we're operating with an identity that isn't true to who we are. We welcome invitations to deconstruction, because they help us change, grow, and become our authentic self.

## A PROCESS OF POSITIVE DISINTEGRATION

Twentieth-century psychologist Kazimierz Dąbrowski called the process of letting go of the status quo of our identities "positive disintegration."[3] Dąbrowski perceived tension, inner conflict, anxiety, depression, and other mental and emotional health issues as part of the process of healing, growing, and becoming one's authentic self. He believed many of our negative conditions and states are necessary growing pains. They're

## 90  Get a Hold of Yourself

not always things we need to cure, fix or treat, because it's only through crisis, suffering, and struggle that we can experience a positive disintegration and evolve.

A positive disintegration is what it sounds like. Your sense of self breaks down and disintegrates, moving you positively in the direction of discovering who you really are. Dąbrowski believed most of us must experience a series of positive disintegrations in our lifetime to become our authentic self.

Positive disintegration is just another way of saying "lose your 'self' to find your self." It's the death and rebirth experience Jesus pointed us to two thousand years ago, when he told us to "pick up our cross daily" (see Matthew 16:24; Mark 8:34; Luke 9:23; 14:27). It's not that we need to experience positive disintegrations daily, but we must remain open and willing to let go of our identities on a regular basis, if we want to know ourselves and be true to ourselves.

## WHO GAVE YOU YOUR IDENTITY?

In the Bible, it didn't take long for human beings to adopt false identities. One of the first questions God asks humanity in the Bible is, "Who told you that?" (See Genesis 3:11.) Who told you that you were naked? That you should be ashamed? That you're unworthy? That you don't measure up and need to hide from me? And why did you believe them?

It's unfortunate, but we all tend to base our identities on things other people have told us. Years ago, one of my spiritual directors, a Trappist monk, stopped me mid-sentence in one of our sessions and said, "You know what your problem is? Once upon a time, somebody told you that you were a scoundrel [he used a cruder term], and you believed them."

His assessment rang true. I'd spent most of my life believing I'm a scoundrel. It never dawned on me, until that moment, that

Identity  *91*

someone else had given me that identity, and I'd accepted it as truth. Author Toni Morrison wrote, "Definitions belong to the definers, not the defined."[4] Other people don't get to define us. They'll try, but you don't have to accept their labels. Only you and your Maker have the authority to define who you are.

After that session, it was like God was saying, "Who told you that, Troy? And why did you believe them? I didn't say that's who you are."

After this, I started to wonder, "Who does God say I am?" This is possibly the most important question we can ask. Many of us never think to ask it because we assume we already know who we are. Because a bunch of imperfect, broken, and at times mean-spirited people, have told us who we are. And we believed them.

## WHO DO YOU SAY I AM?

In the region of Caesarea Philippi, Jesus had an important conversation with his disciples (Matthew 16:13–20; Mark 8:27–30; Luke 9:18–21). He asked them, "Who do people say I am?" After they gave him a few responses, Jesus asked them another question. "Who do you say I am?" Simon answered, "You are the Messiah, the Son of the living God."

One of the reasons Jesus asked his disciples questions about his identity was so they would begin asking the same questions about their own identities. He wanted them to see that the people around us don't know who we really are. That's why he first asked them, "Who do other people say I am?"

They answered, "Some say you're John the Baptist, others say Elijah, some say Jeremiah or one of the prophets." He wanted the disciples to see that other people didn't know his true identity. That the people around us tend to give us identities that aren't true to who we are.

92    **Get a Hold of Yourself**

Next Jesus goes through the same process again, but focuses on Simon's identity this time. Here's my paraphrase of what Jesus says to him:

> Simon. Everyone knows you as Simon. They label you as the son of Jonah. They see you as a fisherman from a fishing family. But they don't know who you really are. I see you are Peter. I see you are blessed and anointed by God. I see you as someone with the keys to the kingdom of heaven, a powerful spiritual leader. And whatever you bind on earth will be bound in heaven, and whatever you loose on earth will be loosed in heaven. (Matthew 16:17–19)

Jesus is trying to help Simon and the other disciples see that the identities other people have given them are not who they really are. Other people see Simon as a fisherman, the son of Jonah, but God sees Simon differently. He sees him as a spiritual leader named Peter. The same is true for us. Only the Spirit of the Most High knows who we really are. This is why Jesus gives Simon a new name, Peter. It's why God gives people like Abraham, Jacob, and Solomon new names in the Bible, to help them understand they have a hidden identity other people can't see. That they usually can't see themselves.

This is a profound story on many levels. In part, it clarifies who Jesus really is. But a major point of this story is that we all need to stop accepting the identities we've been given by others, including our parents and the people who think they know us. Instead, we need to start asking God, "Who do you say I am?"

## WHO DOES GOD SAY YOU ARE?

Our Creator tells us we're God's beloved children, made in the image of God. Many of us have heard this so many times it has lost its impact. Rachel Held Evans writes, "We all long for someone to tell us who we are. The great struggle of the Christian life is to take God's name for us, to believe we are beloved and to believe that is enough."[5] The reason we struggle to believe this identity God has given us, and believe it's enough, is because we need to have an experience of hearing this from God directly, instead of receiving it secondhand.

The dawn of our spiritual awakening is to experience what Jesus experienced at his baptism. To sense the Creator of the Universe saying to us personally, "You are my beloved child, and I am so pleased with you. I take pleasure in who you are." This is what happens when Jesus is baptized in the Spirit, and this is what happens when we're baptized in the Spirit. This doesn't mean you start speaking in tongues (although you might). It means you become aware of God's unconditional love for you, and aware of God's presence with you and within you. When you experience this for yourself, you're reborn.

This is perhaps the most transformative experience we can have. But God wants to reveal even more to us about our hidden identities, as Jesus revealed to Peter. Even more intriguing is that God has given us creative spirits and invites us to be co-creators of our own identities, with God.

## WHITE STONES

In 2012, I visited the personal prayer hermitage of St. Ninian, the first Christian missionary to the Picts in the fifth century. St. Ninian's Cave is in a beautiful and remote area in southwest Scotland. No one was there when I visited. As I enjoyed the solitude, walking along the rocky shoreline of the Irish Sea, I looked down and saw a white stone. A little smaller than the size of a golf ball. I felt mysteriously drawn to it. As I stooped to pick it up, a passage from the book of

94   **Get a Hold of Yourself**

Revelation came to my mind. "To the one who overcomes, . . . I will give them a white stone inscribed with a new name, known only to the one who receives it" (Revelation 2:17, my paraphrase).

I felt like I was standing on holy ground. I felt drenched in sacred love, peace, bliss. I sensed my Creator with me. I stood up and examined the stone, half expecting a name to be written in Hebrew or Aramaic on it. Wouldn't that have been something? Alas, there was nothing. It had no markings or blemishes at all. It was a marvelous, pure white stone. As I stared at it, I realized it was revealing something important to me. My true identity was unknown. It was unknown to the world, to other people, including all the people who thought they knew me. My true identity was a mystery, slowly being revealed in God's appointed time. This was strangely liberating. I felt set free from my past and all my baggage. More than this, I realized my authentic self was still a mystery to me.

## LETTING GO, GROWTH BY SUBTRACTION

This happened thirteen years ago. After this experience, an intense period of letting go began in my life. I underwent a season of positive disintegration. I realized my true identity would not be found in adding more to my life. More accomplishments, titles, degrees, accolades, popularity, success, money, friends, and good deeds. More was not the answer. Discovering and manifesting my authentic self was not about adding but subtracting. Letting go of all the things I'd accumulated, that were not true to who I really am.

There's a quote usually attributed to Antoine de Saint-Exupéry that says, "Perfection is achieved, not when there is nothing more to add, but when there is nothing left to take away." I believe this describes the process of knowing one's authentic self. We don't discover or become our authentic self by adding more, but by letting everything go, until there's nothing left to take away. Shedding all the stuff we've added, and feel we need to add, to be enough. Looking at everything we've been told over the years about who we are and who we should be, and hearing God say, "Who told you that? Who told you that's who you are? Who told you that's who you need to be, to be enough? And why did you believe them?"

Then we must let the Spirit help us let go of it. All of it. And after we let go of everything, we must stay in the void. I realize this sounds daunting. But we must let the emptiness remain and not replace what we've let go of with anything else. This is the only way to be fully open to receive God's insight into who we really are.

Let me explain what I mean by staying in the void. When we crave a cigarette, a sugar binge, pornography, or an online shopping spree, if we choose to not give in to the craving, we often distract ourselves by replacing that activity with something else. We clean the kitchen instead of scrolling social media or chew gum instead of smoking the cigarette. We fill the void, the emptiness we feel, with something else. Which is a very helpful tool to help us kick a bad habit.

If we want to lose ourselves to find ourselves, however, we must let go of everything we identify with and not replace it with anything. This is called *kenosis*, a Greek word that means "self-emptying," used by Paul in Philippians 2:7 to describe Jesus. We must emulate Jesus' self-emptied state to find ourselves.

Kenosis is not easy, and it's impossible to live this way 24-7, but it's in this state of self-emptiness that we give space for the still silent voice of the Spirit to resonate within us.

## RESONATING WITH THE SPIRIT

For a high school science project, I figured out the natural resonant frequency of a crystal glass. I then played that same note or frequency loudly through my guitar amp. To my delight, the crystal glass began to vibrate and "sing" without me touching it. My teacher's capacity to appreciate this amazing feat was overshadowed by his annoyance at the loud piercing sound of my guitar amp, positioned next to the crystal glass I'd placed on his desk. He quickly promised me an A on this project if I would stop.

An easier and less obnoxious way to make a crystal glass "sing" is by rubbing its rim with your wet finger. The note it sings when it is empty is its natural resonant frequency. However, when you add liquid to the crystal glass, it changes the pitch of its resonant frequency. The more liquid you add, the more it changes.

Our inner beings are like a crystal glass. As we fill our inner beings with more stuff, we continually change our resonant frequency, meaning we're out of tune with the natural frequency of the Spirit. For we are made in the image of God, with the same natural resonant frequency as our Creator. The only way to resonate with the Spirit and let God make our inner beings "sing" is to empty the glass of our inner beings. Only then do we restore our natural resonant frequency and attune our hearts to the Spirit.

The Bible tells us the voice of God is like the sound of sheer silence (1 Kings 19:11–13 NRSVue). The natural resonant frequency of God is stillness, silence, emptiness. So we must be still, silent, and empty, to be open and receptive to the Spirit. This is why God encourages us to "be still, and know that I am God" (Psalm 46:10).

Kenosis is emptying ourselves, to return to the natural resonant frequency of the Spirit. This is what I'm convinced Jesus was doing for forty days in the desert. He was entering the spaciousness of inner silence. For forty days and nights, he practiced staying in tune with the natural resonant frequency of the Spirit within himself by tuning out the constant brain-chatter of his human mind.

## SOUND OF SILENCE

I woke up at three a.m. one night, when I was a young father of two rambunctious toddlers. I went downstairs to get a drink of water and was amazed at how quiet it was. I decided to take advantage of the silent night and spend some time in prayer and meditation. I sat down, closed my eyes to "be still and know God," when I noticed the hum of the furnace fan running in the background. I got up and turned it off. I was intent on basking in silence with the Spirit. I sat back down and soon noticed the faint buzz of the refrigerator motor in the kitchen. I was now a man on a mission. I pulled out the fridge and unplugged it. Just for a few minutes, to enjoy complete silence with my Creator. I sat down again and quickly detected the ticking of the clock in the living room. I got up and took the batteries out of the clock. I sat back down and became aware of the distant roar of nighttime traffic on the expressway several miles away.

That's when I had an epiphany. There's so much noise in our external world, we aren't even aware of it, until we take most of the noise away. The same is true internally. There's so much noise within us, so much going on in our hearts and minds, that we're not even aware of it. We're not aware of how many things are competing with the still, silent voice of

98    **Get a Hold of Yourself**

the Spirit within us. It's only as we empty and silence ourselves, one layer at a time, that we become aware of all the background noise within us, drowning out the Spirit within.

As we practice kenosis, as we continue to empty ourselves, we find our inner glass returning closer and closer to the natural resonant frequency of the Spirit within us. We find our soul begins to resonate and "sing" with the Spirit.

How do we do this?

Meditation and silent prayer are what help me empty myself. This isn't about emptying the mind of all our thoughts. That's not possible. It's about keeping my inner awareness empty and clear. To put it another way, it's about focusing my awareness on one thing—the presence of God. As thoughts and feelings come, I notice them, but I don't let my awareness cling to them or be filled with them. I continually return to my awareness of the great I AM.

We can't control what comes in and out of our awareness, but we get to choose what we focus our awareness on. We can focus on the thoughts that pop into our minds, and follow the rabbit trails they lead us down, or we can focus our awareness on being present in the moment with the Spirit.

I find focusing on the breath is a powerful way to keep my focus on the Spirit. The Greek word for breath, *pneuma*, is the same as that for Spirit. In the beginning, humans were brought to life by God breathing into our lungs. Focusing on the breath naturally returns our awareness to God's Spirit, the *pneuma* of life.

The "Yah-weh" prayer has also been helpful for me, to keep my awareness focused on being fully present with God. As I breathe in, I hum "Yah"—and when I exhale, I hum "Weh."

When I attune myself to the Spirit, it's not that God begins talking to me in an audible voice. That's never happened to me. Most of the time, God doesn't use words or ideas to communicate with me. It's simply that my inner glass begins to "sing" with the Spirit. God's "voice" comes as a feeling, sensation, vibration, or "knowing beyond words." The Spirit speaks to us in all kinds of ways, through dreams, Scripture, images, objects, numbers, colors, to name a few. A fun challenge is to read through the Bible and keep a list of all the different ways God communicates with humans. A donkey, a tree set on fire, colored gems, and the ghost of a dead prophet are just a few. I love the creativity and diversity of God's communication with us.

We're all unique people with unique relationships with God, and the Spirit communicates with us in different ways. Yet the Spirit does communicate with us. This we can be certain of. But it requires a certain level of kenosis for us to tune in and hear the still silent voice of the divine.

Embracing kenosis is a lifetime endeavor, but it begins with a prayer practice such as the "Yah-weh" prayer. Choosing something to focus on, to bring our attention back to God's presence. This might be your breath, the name of Jesus, prayer beads, whatever.

## KENOSIS IS LOSING YOUR "SELF"

Ultimately kenosis is a death to self. It's losing ourselves to find ourselves. Emptying ourselves so we can be filled with the Creator Spirit. Exhaling the carbon dioxide, to inhale the life-giving oxygen. The paradoxical point is, *your cup must be emptied, to be filled.*

As mentioned earlier, our expectations are one of the most important things we must surrender and let go of. As a younger pastor, I often prayed "I surrender all," and for the most part I meant it. But I later recognized I had an underlying expectation that God would use me and bless me in certain ways, if I truly surrendered all. This was not true kenosis. I was still clinging to my expectations. We must empty ourselves of everything, even our expectations on God, if we're to be truly open to the Spirit.

## SHED YOUR ROLES

A practice I've found helpful is to release my roles in life. We have a strong tendency to identify with our roles. Mother, husband, carpenter, entrepreneur, the funny guy, the pretty lady, the guy trying to lose weight, the intelligent woman, the fit one, and so on. We all have dozens, if not hundreds of roles in our lives that we identify with. In this practice, I make a list of all my roles, as many as I can think of, and then I let them go. One time I wrote each one on a strip of paper, and burned them, one at a time. Another time I put them in a paper shredder. Releasing them. Emptying my identity from these attachments.

This isn't about releasing our responsibilities. I was releasing my attachments to these roles and responsibilities as my identity, as nouns, that defined my sense of self. I still retained these responsibilities—as verbs.

For example, I accept and honor my responsibility to father my children. But I don't find my identity in being their father. When I find my identity as their father, my fathering role easily becomes possessive. I tend to view these children as mine. In truth, they are not mine, they are God's children. God has entrusted them to me to parent, nurture, and guide, and for me to learn from them. Shifting my perspective this way frees me from the temptation to see my children as extensions of myself, to live vicariously through them or ensure their life choices reflect me in the ways I desire. (As Carl Jung allegedly said, "The greatest burden a child must bear is the unlived life of its parents.") When I'm liberated from identifying with the possessive nature of my roles, such as father, this liberates me to focus on what's best for my children, as God's children. My parenting is no longer about me, my dreams, reputation, or identity.

As I let go of my identification with these various roles, such as father, I empty myself of my identity attachments. This is kenosis.

## BEING FULLY PRESENT

Kenosis is not a one-time event. It's an attitude. A grounding life practice. Continually letting go of everything I attach my identity to, remembering who I am, is an eternal unfolding mystery. Few of us arrive at full kenosis in this lifetime. I certainly haven't. Not even on my best day. Yet practicing kenosis is the example and call of Christ, and it's a powerful practice that helps us live as our authentic self.

I've had profound moments of clarity as I've practiced kenosis over the years and I can say with confidence, when you experience moments of self-emptying and tune in to the natural resonance of the Spirit—you open yourself up to the still silent voice of God. It's hard to put into words how liberating and life-changing it is to sense your Creator interacting with you and making your inner being "sing." It's worth far more than a thousand sermons or books. To know God sees you, notices you, and loves you—as you are. Yet we can only experience God's presence to the degree we're present with God.

Our minds tend to dwell on the past or project into the future. Only by being fully present in the present moment can we experience and be filled with God's presence, because God

## 102  Get a Hold of Yourself

is right here, right now. It's fitting that the first question God asks humanity in the Bible is, "Where are you?" (Genesis 3:9). This is God's call to all of us. "I AM right here, right now. Where are you? Be here with me. Be fully present."

Kenosis is self-emptying, losing ourselves, letting go of our identities or at least holding them loosely. Although this can be daunting, what we discover on the other side of this process is a deeper understanding of who we really are. We discover our authentic self is who we are when we're at home in God, and when God is at home in us. This is the subject of the next chapter.

# 6

# HOME

My brother recently recommended I watch a documentary called *Shiny Happy People*.[1] To say it hit close to home would be an understatement. It started off by focusing on the Duggar family and their popular Christian reality TV show in the 1990s. The real substance of the miniseries, however, was the exposure of Bill Gothard and the impact of his worldwide ministry.

Bill Gothard is a minister and founder of the Institute of Basic Life Principles. Millions of people from around the world have attended Gothard's seminars. He was filling stadiums in the 1970s and 1980s with attendance numbers rivaling the biggest rock concerts. His philosophy of ministry focused on biblical authority, using authoritarian tactics to break the spirits and wills of women and children, essentially brainwashing them into complete submission and obedience. The amount of pain, abuse, and trauma left in the wake of his ministry is incalculable. At the tip of the iceberg are the more than thirty women who have accused Gothard of sexual harassment and molestation.

In the 1980s, I attended Bill Gothard's training seminars along with thousands of other teenagers in Toronto, Ontario. My childhood and adolescent years were immersed in the

## Get a Hold of Yourself

religious fanaticism and authoritarianism of his toxic brand of Christianity. I've had to work through a tremendous amount of baggage because of my religious upbringing. I understand why people walk away from the church and Christianity. I know the dark side of religion all too well.

## PARTING IS SUCH SWEET SORROW

In my early twenties, I left the church and abandoned my Christian faith. Even though it had been "home" my entire life, I left the fundamentalist world of my upbringing because it was an abusive, dysfunctional, and intolerable place to live. I now refer to it as the OTR (old time religion). As strange as it might sound, after I left the OTR, I couldn't conceive of anything else being home either, as far as faith and spirituality were concerned. For most of my twenties I wandered, spiritually homeless.

This wilderness period was essential to my growth journey. My faith was dying, and a new faith was being born in me. This took time and a lot of letting go. During my agnostic years, I remained haunted by the OTR. I abhorred its domineering and debilitating belief system, but I frequently felt a lingering conviction to return to it, so I could get right with God. I was still convinced that to "get right with God," I had to return to the OTR. The faith I'd come to despise as irrational, abusive, and repulsive. Because I still believed it was home. A dysfunctional and toxic home, a place I could never go back to, but home, nonetheless. Finding a new spiritual home or path to reconnect with God seemed inconceivable. The OTR tentacles ran deep in my psyche. I believed all other paths were heresy, worldly, or worse, demonic. So instead of finding a new spiritual path, I wandered in the wilderness.

Shedding the fundamentalist Christian skin I was born with was a long and tedious journey. It left me feeling ashamed, confused, and lost. Although the yoke of Christian religiosity wrapped around my neck was not easy to bear, and its burden was anything but light, I was afraid to permanently leave it behind. This is what happens when the threat of hell is embedded in your psyche from a young age. My church claimed to be scaring hell out of us kids, but they were embedding the fear of hell into us. Consequently, I know how difficult and frightening it is to shake oneself free of one's religious programming. It's a transition that involves replacing the very foundation underneath one's feet. What could be more unsettling than that?

I believe this religious deprogramming process is especially challenging for people like me. For people who've encountered the loving Creator in the context of our dysfunctional and toxic religious upbringing. It's a complicated, confusing, and painful journey to leave the home through which we first met the Most High. Because it feels like we're abandoning God.

## ABANDONERS, ADHERENTS, AGITATORS, AFFILIATED, AND ADAPTORS

Many ex-Christians I know are what I call "abandoners." If that sounds judgmental, that's not my intention. I'm trying to describe their religious deprogramming succinctly.

These are people who grew up as Christians, in the church, but at some point, chose to throw off the shackles of all the "God stuff" and faith completely. That's how they came to view the Christian faith of their upbringing, as nonsense, a prison, or both. Letting go was easy for them. They wanted nothing to do with it anymore. It had no value for them. So, they abandoned it and never looked back.

It's not as easy for those of us who experienced something real, beautiful, and life-giving in our Christian faith, alongside

*106* **Get a Hold of Yourself**

the negative, destructive, and unreasonable elements. For us it feels like letting go of both the burden and the blessing.

There's another group I call "adherents." Some of these people came to faith later in life and have no baggage with the church or faith. Some of them were raised in the church but never felt a need to leave the Christian faith they were born into. Some of them stay because they're still under the spell of their childhood religious programming. However, many stay because their childhood faith was positive and meaningful. It was and continues to be a safe and nurturing spiritual home for them.

Not only do I respect adherents, I envy them. It seems like a much easier journey. Both adhering and abandoning are relatively straightforward approaches to faith.

There's a third group I call the "agitated." The agitated don't abandon or adhere to their faith, they critique it and complain about it. The hard core agitated like to stir the pot and rock the boat. They tend to rehash the same old issues, like Jesus' divinity, the inerrancy of Scripture, church scandals, or church politics, but they never seem to change anything, including themselves. They just keep swirling around the same old toilet bowl of deconstruction, never flowing down into the sewers, into the underworld of death to "self," where their questions and doubts should take them. That's one of the purposes of our questions and doubts. To take us to a place of releasing the beliefs we no longer need, and experience death and rebirth.

Instead of letting go of their beliefs, the agitated hold on to their questions, doubts, and critiques, as a person lost at sea clings to a lifeboat. They cling to their questions and doubts the same way fundamentalists cling to their beliefs and doctrine. The agitated are fundamentalists, only their dogma is doubt.

Doubts and questions are important. Essential, I'd argue. But the only way to let your unanswerable questions and unresolvable doubts do their work is to let them "drown" you. Our doubts often play an important role in our death to "self." If it feels like they are destroying your belief system, they are. But this is part of the growth process. Our beliefs often become idols in our lives. It's only as we surrender our image of God, the "god" who fits inside our finite brains, that we can experience the infinite God who transcends the capacity of our minds to comprehend. Only then can we experience spiritual rebirth. This requires tremendous courage and faith.

However, we're not brave for clinging to our doubts or endlessly questioning the beliefs and certainties we were raised with, or those held by the people around us. When we become stuck in perpetual deconstruction, it's because we're afraid. Afraid of death. Yet it's only through death that we can experience new life, a renewed faith and deeper relationship with our Creator.

Some of the agitated leave church and judge Christianity and the church from the outside. They often become bitter or resentful, in my experience. Others find a new church every few years, to challenge a new audience with their "greatest hits" of questions and concerns. These cynical souls are often quite clever and fun to converse with, in small doses. After a while I find them exhausting, though, because they're not looking for answers. They're looking for more evidence, ammunition, and reasons to keep doubting, questioning, critiquing, and complaining. For this has become their comfort zone. I know these people well, because I was one of them, for years. I still have relapses, occasionally.

There's a fourth group I call the "affiliated." These people have what you might call a part-time or arm's length connection to church and faith. Some of them are hyphenated Christians such as new age–Christians or secular–Christians. They hold many Christian beliefs and values but it doesn't always seem to be the center of their lifestyle, practices, or worldview, at least on the surface.

Some of them have plugged in to church later in life or reconnected with church and faith as adults. Some have maintained some degree of connection since childhood. They tend to say things like, "I just don't think about it too much" or "Church is more about a sense of community for me" or "It was important for us to raise our children with Christian values."

In my younger years, I used to judge these affiliates as lukewarm or wishy-washy Christians. I'm fascinated by them now. As I get older, I see the wisdom in their choice to:

1. Not waste time worrying about mysteries they can't comprehend;
2. Refrain from getting bothered by things they can't, or won't, change;
3. Avoid questions that don't really have answers; and
4. Engage church and faith at a level that's meaningful for them.

I may not always understand their connection with God or faith, but I no longer judge or question them. They're one of the groups I learn the most from currently.

The final group are the adapters. These people are adapting and changing as they let go of their old framework of faith, to experience God and life with new eyes or a new state of consciousness. Faith has become a transformation process for these people. This process is often messy because adapters have often experienced something real, beautiful, and life-giving in their childhood faith, alongside the negative, destructive, and unreasonable elements. They remember many good things about their old home, but they also recognize it's uninhabitable now. So, they adapt to a new home, or to the adventure they're being invited on to explore new and unfamiliar territory, as spiritual nomads.

By adapting, I don't mean adjusting to the contemporary convictions and opinions of their cultural context or twenty-first century experiences. I mean adapting to the movement of the Spirit and the call within them to trust God to guide them home. Their true home. This often means leaving home, where their tribe has resided for years, decades, or longer. This was no small task for Abram and Sarai when God called them to leave their homeland of Ur, forsaking their family, friends, culture, and tribe, to journey into an unknown land, with new identities as Abraham and Sarah (see Genesis 12:1–3). It's no small task for us today either. It means walking away from all we've known, at least for a season. It sometimes involves being perceived as confused, lost, backslidden, heretical, or rebellious against God, by the religious people who knew us. For others it means being judged and mocked for becoming a religious nutjob by the nonreligious people in our lives.

## THE WAY LEADS THROUGH THE WILDERNESS

No matter what our faith looks like, the way to the Promised Land usually leads us through the wilderness at some point. This can feel like we've made a wrong turn somewhere. You probably haven't. The wilderness is part of the journey. Author Sarah Bessey reminds us, "You have ended up in the wilderness, not in spite of your faithfulness, but because of it."[2] Spiritual homelessness, the way of the nomad, is the only path to Canaan for many of us.

*110* **Get a Hold of Yourself**

It doesn't matter if we grew up in a religious home or not. It doesn't matter if the church we grew up in was nurturing or toxic and abusive. All our journeys will require us to leave some aspect of home at some point, to find our true home. We'll be required to step outside of our comfort zones and the shadow of our past, to be reborn. Again. And sometimes, again.

## PRODIGAL SON

Jesus tells a story called the parable of the prodigal son (Luke 15:11–32), where the youngest son asked his wealthy dad for his part of the inheritance, while his father was still alive. His dad was hurt by this, naturally, but he agreed. The son took the money and ran. He traveled to a far-off country and blew it all, living large. He partied hard. It didn't take long till he'd spent all the money. It wasn't long after that till he hit rock bottom. He learned how hard life could be. He came to understand firsthand the injustice and suffering of life. He experienced betrayal, dishonesty, abandonment, being taken advantage of, and all the other harsh realities of this "dog eat dog" world. His so-called friends had forsaken him, now that he had nothing to offer them. He found himself alone, poor, and hungry, working for an unfair boss, doing hard labor, unable to make ends meet. He went dumpster diving in a pig trough to find food to eat. As he contemplated eating the slop in the pig trough, he hit an all-time low. Yet that's where he experienced a breakthrough.

Jesus said it was here he "came to his senses" (Luke 15:17). He began to see clearly, perhaps for the first time. Up until this point, he'd been blinded by assumptions, expectations, greed, baggage, wishful thinking, naive optimism, anger, resentment, entitlement, self-pity, the kinds of things that blind us all.

It was in this rock-bottom moment he found clarity. This is often the way.

After this moment of clarity, he decided to return home to ask his dad for forgiveness and request a job on the family farm. He didn't expect his dad to accept him as a son again. He realized how disrespectful and hurtful he'd been, but he knew his father was a fair man, who would at least pay a fair wage. He returned home and much to his surprise, he was not only forgiven and accepted back into the family. He came to see the home he'd left was the promised land he'd been looking for all along.

There are many levels to this story, but ultimately, it's about how we all journey home. The son thought his journey to freedom was about going to a faraway land to find heaven on earth. Yet his story was about the long journey he had to take through the unknown wilderness, to return to the place where he started, and see it with new eyes. To discover it was the paradise he'd been looking for all along.

Of course, he couldn't see and experience his home as heaven on earth until he first left it, seeking the promised land elsewhere. This is true for all of us, on some level. Poet T. S. Eliot says, "We shall not cease from exploration, and the end of all our exploring will be to arrive where we started and know the place for the first time."[3]

I've lost count of the number of people who've told me they had to leave their Christian faith in order to return to it later on, rediscovering its truth and beauty on a deeper level. To return where they started, and find it was the very home they'd been searching for.

For those of you who came to faith later in life, it might be hard to relate to the prodigal son. But you too have left home.

## 112  Get a Hold of Yourself

We are all born as children of God, with a relationship with God. You might not remember it, but you walked away from your Creator. We all have, thousands of times in our lives. We've rejected God's bids for connecting with us more deeply and directly, countless times. We've all abandoned our home in God, one way or another.

For those of you who've never left home, who've never questioned or abandoned your faith or relationship with God, you too might struggle to relate to the prodigal son. Well, the story includes you as well. Unfortunately, you might be the older son who never left and consequently struggled to fully receive and experience God's love. If your faith is exactly the same as it was when you were a child, you're probably overdue for a walk in the wilderness.

## MEETING CHRIST IN THE WILDERNESS

The importance of leaving home is a truth some Christians can't appreciate or understand. For them, it feels sinful or wrong to leave, especially if they've been programmed from a young age or are prone to guilt or being loyal to a fault. Yet it's important to understand that it was in unfamiliar territory where the prodigal son came to his senses.

One of the most heartbreaking aspects of the prodigal son story is that the older brother, who tried to be faithful and loyal, never left home, and never experienced a breakthrough. He was unable to find the promised land of love, peace, and fulfillment that the prodigal son found. At some point, he too may have to leave home to find home.

It was in my wilderness wandering, far from home, that I came to my senses. The journey that brought me back to Christ included a rock-bottom experience. A few of them. In my early twenties I began self-medicating and soon found myself on a self-destructive path. I was no longer the life of the party. I was on a bad path, bringing pain and chaos to myself and those around me. My girlfriend of six years left me, my friendships dwindled, my band fell apart, and my dream of becoming a successful musician died. Penniless and alone, I traded in my guitar and music equipment at a pawn shop to buy more "medicine" to numb my pain and loneliness. Like the prodigal son, I felt abandoned. Even God had abandoned me, I assumed, because I'd abandoned my faith.

One night, I was so desperate and weary of the path I was on, I decided to pray. To my surprise, God came running down the road to embrace me with open arms, just like the father with the prodigal son. I felt enveloped in God's love, grace, and forgiveness. Soon after that, God brought the right people into my life to help me get on a new path.

Besides bringing me to several rock-bottom moments, my journey in the wilderness also included experiences that enlightened me to see Christ in new ways, that I wouldn't have been able to see, if I'd never left the OTR. In my season of agnosticism, I explored other philosophies, spiritualities, and wisdom traditions and met Christ beyond the confines of my religious programming. For example, I came across a poem by a Sufi poet named Ḥāfiz, who wrote, "I am a hole in a flute that the Christ's breath moves through—listen to this music."[4] This poem hit me. I felt healing. I sensed Divine Presence around me. Something in these words resounded so loudly with truth, it melted the resistance and rigid defenses of my heart. It opened me up to the Spirit of Christ again.

Several other moments like this happened during my wandering years, where I encountered Christ in surprising places and people, in profound and transformative ways. These experiences helped me develop a spiritual sensitivity and a new lens that enabled me to see through the abuse, baggage, and trauma of my childhood church and faith, to see the depth of riches to be found in Christ and Christian spirituality. It was important that these encounters happened outside the church and Christianity for me. I'm not sure I would have been able to receive this message from a Christian or a church during my recovery years. Yet eventually, I heard the voice of one calling in the wilderness (see Isaiah 40:3 and John 1:23), calling me back home. Not to my childhood church, faith, or fundamentalist belief system, but back home to Christ.

## RETURNING HOME

Some people meet Christ in the wilderness as adults and then join the church. For them, joining a church is like finally finding home. Some people, like my wife, met Christ in the church as a child and have no church baggage at all. Then there are the people like me. I'd like to speak directly to those who have been burned by the church in their youth.

We need to see Christ is not confined to the rigid religiosity that hurt us. I believe this was one of the great sins of my childhood church. They tried to make God and Jesus small enough to fit into their religious package. They acted like God, Christ, and truth belonged to them, like possessions they owned and could use to control others. The abusive and authoritarian OTR I was raised in was steeped in illusion, deception, manipulation, and control. Yet it was also rooted in something real and true. My journey in the wilderness gave me the experience and tools I needed to dig beneath the surface of my childhood religion, to find the hidden treasure buried underneath it. It's important to clarify that I returned to the treasure, not to the dirt it was buried in.

**Home**  *115*

In the wilderness I received the tools of humility, compassion, forgiveness, openness, and objectivity. I was able to see I was as messed up as the religious people who hurt me in my youth. I was able to see they were hurting too. I came to understand that hurt people, hurt people. I learned how to ask better questions. Instead of asking, "What's wrong with those people?" I learned to ask, "What happened to those people? What wounds, fear, trauma, and issues caused them to act that way?" I learned to not throw the baby out with the bathwater. I learned to see that God's unconditional love and grace make God willing to work with imperfect and flawed people. This is why the church is full of imperfect and hurtful people. People like you and me.

When I say the Spirit often leads those of us burned by the church to return home, I don't mean we'll return to the same church, people, or belief systems that wounded or misled us. Returning home isn't about going back to religion, it's about entering a deeper level of faith we might call spirituality. It's not about going back to the same people or community that wounded us. It's about finding and entering new (or rekindling old) spiritual relationships, and reconnecting with a new spiritual community, because we understand how important healthy relationships and genuine community are to our own growth and well-being. Returning home isn't about going back to the old ways of reading and understanding the Bible, it's about returning to Scripture and divine wisdom with a new perspective, that seeks to understand the deeper hidden meaning in everything that reveals God's truth and love. Returning home isn't about returning to a particular set of doctrines, it's about returning to a unique and intimate relationship with God. It's about opening ourselves up to the love and authority

## 116  Get a Hold of Yourself

of our Creator, the guidance of the Holy Spirit, and the teachings of Jesus.

Although returning home may include returning to some of the things we left behind, how we interact with "the things of old" will be new and different, because we're new and different. This is why leaving is so important. It changes us and our perspective. It's rare for someone to experience this transformation, this shift in consciousness, if they never leave home. It's difficult to "come to our senses" and develop a new or heightened spiritual sensitivity, if we're like the older brother and never leave the old and familiar. To receive new insight and new treasure from the "things of old," we must develop a new mindset, new wineskins.

This usually requires a transformative journey in the wilderness. If it was necessary for Jesus, it's necessary for us. However, most of us will require more than forty days in the wilderness.

For some of us, leaving home is leaving the church. For some of us, leaving home may be leaving a relationship, a job, a mindset, or an affiliation with a political party. At some point the Spirit will nudge us all out of our comfort zones. Beyond our limits into uncharted territory.

If you've never left home and gone through a period of wandering, you might be resisting the call of the Spirit in your life. Or it may simply not be your time. However, it's inevitable. If you want to grow spiritually, you'll have to go on a journey that takes you away from "home," outside your comfort zone. This is the way.

Ironically, our path often leads us back to the place we started, with new eyes, to find the treasure buried beneath the surface. But it's the journey, the leaving, that equips us with the new eyes to find this hidden treasure. This might be

## Home   117

leaving and returning to the church, or a complicated relationship with a parent, or revisiting wounds we've suppressed for years or a skeleton in our personal or familial closet. A returning or revisiting of some kind will be required to find healing and wholeness.

This applies to our faith journey, but it applies to our life journey in general. One of the most difficult tasks of personal growth is to feel at home in our own skin. To find the treasure in who we are, as we are. To be comfortable being ourselves, in all contexts, circumstances, and settings. We spend much of our lives trying to fit in, to be what others expect us to be. What our parents, peers, pastors, professors, professional idols, personal heroes, and any other people you can think of that start with the letter P, expect us to be. As a result, we often end up trying to be someone we're not. Not only because we don't know who we are, but because we don't always like who we perceive ourselves to be.

Many of us wish we had different bodies, that are leaner, more evenly proportioned, or more muscular. We desire faces that are less round or with higher cheekbones or different shaped chins. We wish we had thicker hair, straighter hair, or any hair at all. We desire different minds with higher IQs, different hearts with higher EQs, different personalities, sexual orientations, skills, gifts, abilities, charisma, qualities, and traits. We wish we had more passion or less passion.

These "wishes" take us on a wilderness journey. Leaving the "home" of who we are, to seek out the promised land elsewhere, trying to be someone else. Someone we're not. This isn't a bad thing. It's a natural part of our personal growth process. We must leave home to return home and see our "self" with new eyes. Yet eventually, we'll be called to return home. To be ourselves. Our authentic self.

## 118  Get a Hold of Yourself

Returning home is ultimately about seeing who we are with a new lens or different state of consciousness, enabling us to be at home in our own skin. To embrace the unique individuals we are, with all our particularities, peculiarities, and limitations. To be at home in our own mind, heart, body, personality, and experiences. To see the treasure that our authentic self really is. To see paradise isn't found out there somewhere, in being more like someone else. The promised land we're seeking is found within. Returning home is discovering and manifesting who we really are, fully and freely.

This usually only happens after a journey of wandering, spending years or decades trying to find our true home in a faraway land, out there somewhere. Eventually we realize we won't find it out there. We realize it's not the responsibility of others to make us feel at home. This is something we must do for ourselves. And this requires a profound inner journey that helps us "come to our senses."

Author Brené Brown often refers to her "breakdown" as a breakthrough and spiritual awakening.[5] We don't all need a breakdown or rock-bottom moment per se, but we all need a transformative moment. A moment or process that creates a shift in our consciousness, where new wineskins are created within us. Jesus emphasizes this for good reason, for only with new eyes and renewed perspectives are we able to find the buried treasure in our own lives. To see the deeper truth and beauty in our own hearts, minds, bodies, and souls. To see we'll never arrive at the promised land by being someone else.

Don't judge yourself if you're wandering or struggling to accept yourself as you are. You're on a journey that will eventually lead you to a transformative moment. However, transformation doesn't happen all at once. The spiritual journey is a spiral movement with many transformative moments. It involves revisiting the same places, again and again, from different vantage points and perspectives. The path of spiritual growth is a spiral not a circle. It's an ascending or descending cycle. On this spiral movement of growth, we never revisit the same place from the same altitude or position, but we constantly revisit the same places, wounds, issues, and needs from different altitudes and angles. This is why we don't just pick up our cross and die to self once. We experience death and rebirth multiple times as we grow spiritually.

Like Brené Brown and the prodigal son, we'll experience low points on our journeys, which are actually breakthroughs, if we let them break through our resistance to transformation. These transformative moments are moments of grace. We can't make them happen though. They come upon us in unexpected ways, places, and times. We can't plan or schedule them, but we can miss them or resist them when they do happen. One of the purposes of our spiritual disciplines is to prepare us for these moments, to be open and receptive when they come. This is why it's so important to practice kenosis and be fully present in every season, especially the difficult ones.

Our journeys of leaving and finding home will look different for all of us, but when our moment of grace in the wilderness comes, and we receive it, we'll find we're already at home, right where we are. In the bodies we inhabit, with the personalities we've been given. With the God we've been seeking, who is also seeking us. We discover we've been home all along; we just didn't have eyes to see it. As Jacob exclaims in the wilderness, "Surely God is in this place, I just wasn't aware of it until now!" (Genesis 28:16, my translation). This is spiritual awakening. To realize God is with us, always. And whenever God is with us, we are at home.

7

# SNAKES

I was ready to quit. I'd had enough of church politics and drama. A colleague of mine had quit ministry a few years earlier and started a business. He said he'd never been happier. He told me the business world was way less vicious than dealing with some church people. This sounded appealing. I was ready for a change.

I met with my Trappist monk spiritual director and told him I was thinking of quitting. I'll never forget what he said. "You can do that. But then I'd have to punch you in the face." Talk about an unexpected response! After I recovered from the shock, he smiled and continued. "Because you obviously need to learn how to take a punch! I've seen too many good ministers quit when it gets tough. Did you think it was going to be easy? When things get tough, you have to get tougher. You need to develop thick skin to deal with people. Especially religious people. This is a growth opportunity for you. Stop trying to be nice and start being real. Stop being a dove all the time and be a serpent once in a while."

I believe the reason I'm still a pastor today is because of that conversation. He helped me see several things in a different light. Including Jesus' command to be like a serpent.

## 122    Get a Hold of Yourself

I'd never understood Jesus' command for us to be snake-like and dove-like. They're about as opposite as two animals can be. How can we be like both? I think most Christians struggle with this on some level. Being dove-like makes sense but being snake-like—that doesn't add up. The Bible teaches us to be wary of snakes. Genesis tells us the serpent was at the root of humanity's departure from the garden (Genesis 3). Yet Jesus instructs his followers to be savvy as serpents and pure as doves (see Matthew 10:16). What does Jesus have in mind here?

From a psychological and spiritual growth perspective, I think Jesus is saying we must embrace our paradoxical nature as human beings. To be whole, we must integrate our opposites. One way of simplifying the complexity of human nature is to say we have a serpent side and a dove side. Jesus is inviting us to integrate both because he doesn't want us to be so heavenly minded, we're no earthly good. Nor does he want us to be so worldly wise we can't see and serve the kingdom of heaven. We must be worldly wise and spiritually awakened to be our authentic self.

There's a reason Jesus mentions becoming savvy as serpents first though. Before we can effectively integrate our dove side, we must integrate our serpent side. We must develop a clear, healthy, and independent sense of self before we can effectively die to self. This is called ego differentiation in Jungian psychology, and it's the first major task of our psychological development.

In short, integrating our serpent side is about developing worldly wisdom and a healthy ego that is capable and competent to survive and thrive on our own. It is learning to take responsibility for our lives, face our fears, and develop self-confidence. It's learning to rely on ourselves, knowing we're capable of meeting the challenges and adversity of life. A

**Snakes** *123*

healthy ego enables us to establish a distinct personal identity, separate from our family, tribe, and society. This process is what I call the serpent journey. It begins with facing our fears.

## HERE BE DRAGONS

Some medieval mapmakers wrote the inscription "here be dragons" on unexplored territories on maps. The ongoing popularity of the phrase "here be dragons" in film, fantasy novels, legend, and folklore, reveals something interesting about the human psyche. We have a fearful fascination with what exists in the unknown. The unknown world is a hostile and dangerous place in our imaginations, because the world we know and inhabit is a hostile and dangerous place.

According to the World Health Organization, "One person commits suicide every 40 seconds, one person is murdered every 60 seconds, and one person dies in armed conflict every 100 seconds."[1] This isn't a description of an imaginary world in some dystopian film. This is the world we live in. Jesus confirms our fears that the world is a violent and dangerous place when he says we're like lambs among wolves in this world. He says we'll suffer, have trouble, and endure trials and tribulations. He says people will betray, persecute, and abuse us.

What intensifies our fear and anxiety is that we can't always predict who our betrayers and abusers will be. We see in Jesus' life that it is often the people closest to us who hurt us the most. Like his friend Judas who betrayed him, or the people he grew up with who tried to throw him off a cliff when he preached a sermon they didn't like. This is why Jesus encourages us to watch out for "wolves in sheep's clothing" (Matthew 7:15). Some people are not what they appear or claim to be. They might seem nice on the surface but inside they're ravenous predators.

## 124 **Get a Hold of Yourself**

Jesus laments that children tend to suffer the most in our world. He says, "It would be better to tie a large concrete block around the necks of those who harm children, and throw them into the sea, then to let them continue harming children" (see Luke 17:2). Jesus sounds more like a mafia boss here than a gentle shepherd. This is how seriously he's offended and disturbed by the mistreatment of children.

Jesus understands most of us begin to live with fear from a young age. We incur our deepest wounds as children, because this is when we're most vulnerable. This is why so many children's stories, fairy tales, and songs focus on monsters and scary things. They are preparing our young psyches for our inevitable encounters with scary monsters in reality.

## YOU CAN'T STAY IN THE GARDEN FOREVER

The only place the Bible says a child can play with snakes and not be harmed is in the kingdom of heaven, as described in Isaiah 11.

> In that day the wolf and the lamb will live together;
>> the leopard will lie down with the baby goat.
> The calf and the yearling will be safe with the lion,
>> and a little child will lead them all.
> The cow will graze near the bear.
>> The cub and the calf will lie down together. . . .
> The baby will play safely near the hole of a cobra.
>> Yes, a little child will put its hand in a nest of deadly
>> snakes without harm.
> (Isaiah 11:6–9 NLT)

This is a prophetic description of a world that has returned to a state of innocence. Where the purity of all things has been restored under the benevolent rule of the Creator, like it was in the garden of Eden. This is a reality we all long for, at least subconsciously. I suspect this is why we're drawn to beautiful gardens, parks, and scenic nature areas. It's why we take vacations in exotic coastal areas and islands, in places that are insulated from the "real world" full of problems, hardship, ugliness, and suffering. We're drawn to places that resemble idyllic gardens of paradise, where everything is beautiful and safe, because we have an ambiguous homesick longing to return to our garden of innocence.

This garden of innocence Isaiah describes is our initial reality as children. If you watch young children play, their toy wolves and lambs are usually friends. Their lions and goats go on adventures together and look out for one another. The chicken on their dinner plates isn't the same chicken as the quirky animal in the friendly farmer's barnyard. It couldn't be.

Yet children eventually realize life feeds on life. We all come to understand wolves eat lambs, leopards eat baby goats, and humans eat chickens. We see the world is not a garden of innocence, it's a violent and dangerous place, where bees sting, snakes bite, bullies are real, friends can be cruel, parents disappoint us, and loved ones hurt us. This realization forces us out of our garden of innocence. We leave our peaceful paradise, where the world seemed safe and wonderful. Usually at a very young age. Sometimes abruptly, by a painful or traumatic experience.

In Genesis, young Adam and Eve live in this garden of innocence, where there's no horror, abuse, suffering, tragedy, violence, or trauma. They live here until their eyes are opened to see the world is not only good. They see there's both good *and* evil in the world. Not everything is rosy and nice. There are dangerous and deceitful snakes in the world. There's another part of reality, outside the garden of Eden,

## Get a Hold of Yourself

full of thistles, hardship, pain, adversity, and danger. Where humans must toil and struggle to survive.

Adam and Eve's story is our story. None of us stay in our garden of innocence forever. Our eyes are eventually opened to see the world is filled with both good *and* evil. We're awakened to dualistic thinking. We're exiled from the garden and wake up to an entirely different reality, where "there be dragons." And snakes. This is when our serpent journey begins.

## DWELLING IN A SNAKE-FILLED LAND

Jesus encourages us to approach the serpent paradoxically. We must be wary of snakes, while also learning from them and becoming more like them. On the one hand, pretending that snakes don't exist or that they're not dangerous is naive. Our serpent journey is about moving away from our naive childishness and becoming worldly-wise adults. The world will eat us alive if we stay naive. On the other hand, one of the ways we learn how to survive in a snake-filled land is by becoming more snake-like.

There's a fascinating story in the book of Numbers (21:4–9). The Hebrews had left Egypt after being held in captivity for four hundred years and were being led by God to the promised land. Their journey through the wilderness lasted forty years, a voyage that should have taken around twelve days, if they'd traveled a direct route. The first thing this story teaches us about our journey to the promised land is that it will take longer than we think.

The Hebrews began complaining about how difficult and dangerous the journey had become. Then things went from bad to worse. They found themselves in a snake-filled land. Venomous serpents started attacking them. Many of them got

Snakes   127

sick from the bites. Some of them died. Understandably, they cried out to God to rescue them.

This is where the story takes a surprising twist. God didn't destroy the snakes or lead the Hebrews out of this snake-filled region. Instead, God instructed them to make a bronze serpent and mount it on a pole. When people were bitten by a snake, God told them to look up to the bronze serpent. When they did, they recovered.

It's a weird story but it contains profound truth. In our own personal development, we're often surprised how hard, unfair, and dangerous the road to the promised land is. Like the Hebrews and the prodigal son, we hope to travel to paradise as quickly as possible, to enjoy the high life on easy street, in a land flowing with milk and honey. This isn't how most of our lives unfold though. We're usually surprised and disappointed at how difficult and arduous the journey becomes. We complain and insist reality shouldn't be the way it is. We try to retain our innocence, crying out, "I'm innocent. I don't deserve to be treated this way. This isn't fair. Life shouldn't be like this. Why are there so many snakes, biting, betraying, undermining, and hurting me?"

In between our complaining, we ask God to rescue us from this snake-filled land. We naively expect God to transform reality to adapt to us, rather than help us adapt to reality. We're shocked to learn the way we survive is not by getting rid of the snakes or escaping the snake filled land. The solution is, much to our surprise, by looking up to the serpent.

In a garden, Jesus prays and asks to be spared the pain and turmoil of the cross. The symbolism seems obvious. He wants to stay in the garden and avoid the pain and suffering ahead of him. The answer to his prayer is the answer we get as well. We must endure the cross, not escape it. To be clear, the Bible doesn't encourage us to look for crosses to bear, or snake-filled caves to enter. Yet when our path leads us to a cross or a cave, there's rarely a magical or miraculous escape route around them. We must pass through them. We must bear our cross and enter our caves. When we do, we come out stronger, braver, and wiser on the other side. This is the serpent journey.

The way to growth, freedom, and maturity is not by escaping the intimidating serpents all around us, but by looking up to them, learning from them, and adopting some of their positive traits. When we accept this, we begin our serpent journey.

## LEARNING FROM UNLIKELY SOURCES

A snake is an unlikely creature for Jesus to encourage us to emulate. So too, some of the people we'll need to learn from on our serpent journeys will be unexpected. Our initial reactions to them may resemble our reaction to snakes. We'll be apprehensive, nervous, or even repulsed by the way they conduct themselves. If you're a gentle, sensitive, and spiritual person, admiring and learning from bold, confident, and decisive people will likely take you out of your comfort zone. That's in part why we need to do it.

Maybe you have an overly ambitious co-worker who keeps getting promotions, or a super confident cousin who commands every room they enter, or an extremely assertive friend who always seems to get what they want, or a fanatically disciplined acquaintance at the gym you cross paths with twice a week. These people are not snakes, to be clear, but they often hold "serpent wisdom" we can learn from. They might come across as arrogant, self-centered, or off-putting to us at first. But sometimes we need these unlikely mentors, who are worldly-wise, independent, and strong, to help us develop healthy egos.

We must be cautious and discerning though. It's tricky business to be wary of serpent traits while simultaneously admiring them and learning from them. On the one hand, we must be attentive to not lose our sensitivity to the Spirit as we take our serpent journeys and learn to be confident, courageous, and assertive. On the other hand, we can't let our fear prevent us from learning from unlikely people who can help us realize our potential.

Many Christians feel obligated to be gentle, compassionate, and servant-hearted and don't know how to reconcile their desires to be bold, assertive, resilient, and confident. Jesus is letting us know we don't have to be one or the other. We can be both. Jesus was no pushover, and he doesn't call us to be pushovers. Jesus was courageous, strong, and assertive. Yet he was aligned with the Spirit and compassionate towards people, especially the most vulnerable in our midst.

If you can find someone who embodies strength, confidence, and assertiveness, as well as compassion, sensitivity, and spiritual maturity, you have found an ideal mentor. Many of us will struggle to find such a mentor. We may have to learn the way of the serpent from worldly-wise people, who may not embody the spiritual maturity we also aim to develop. We will need a variety of mentors and teachers, some who are spiritually awakened and some who are worldly-wise.

Sometimes it's best to separate these two schools in our lives, because sometimes strong, confident, assertive people who claim to be spiritually mature are actually wolves in sheep's clothing. They can do more damage than good. Sometimes it's cleaner to separate our serpent wisdom learning from our dove learning. When you're focused on learning "serpent wisdom" from a worldly-wise person, you're not expecting them to also teach you how to worship, pray, or forgive. You're clear on what you're trying to learn from them, while you're seeking spiritual growth training from different mentors.

To put it another way, we don't need our math tutor to be a spiritually mature person to teach us calculus. I've learned much about worldly wisdom from Stoic philosophy, for example, but I don't expect it to teach me how to be attuned with the Spirit. There is worldly wisdom we can learn from people who aren't spiritually awakened. This is, in part, what Jesus is implying by telling us to learn from snakes. Not that these worldly-wise people are snakes. Let me be clear about that. Jesus' point is we may need to learn from unlikely sources.

However, I also think Jesus is telling us to learn from actual snakes.

## THE WAY OF THE SERPENT

According to anthropologist Lynne Isbell and her "snake detection theory," snakes had a major influence on the evolutionary improvement of eyesight in primates.[2] This theory is the subject of debate in the scientific community, but she's right about one thing. Humans have unique and instinctive responses to snakes and anything resembling a snake. Have you ever jolted at the sight of a stick or rope that kind of looked a snake?

We're subconsciously looking for snakes around every corner, which makes us vigilant, attentive, and aware of our surroundings. This is a gift. Being oblivious and inattentive is a sure way to get stung or bit by things we should have noticed and could have avoided. Being inattentive is a great way to get mugged, manipulated, scammed, or taken advantage of. Knowing there are snakes around, and that some of them are dangerous, not only makes us pay attention, it motivates us to learn, discover, and develop tools and techniques to help us detect threats, avoid danger, and defend ourselves.

We can learn a lot from actual snakes, because snakes are survivors. They've learned how to thrive in this perilous world. One of the survival skills we learn from snakes is to be subtle, lay low, and adapt. There's a time to be bold and outspoken, but we must pick our battles carefully. The best way to avoid trouble is to not attract unwanted attention to ourselves. Learn to hold your tongue. Don't rock the boat and ruffle feathers. Be like the snake. Snakes don't go looking for trouble. They avoid trouble. They're masters of camouflage and blending in, when they need to. Sometimes it's important to stand out, but it's important to learn how to blend in.

Snakes thrive in almost any setting because they learn how to adapt to their surroundings. They're one of the most successful animals on the planet as far as survival and adaptation go. They exist in almost every country, climate, and terrain on earth. They've learned to thrive in deserts, mountains, forests, jungles, islands, swamps, grasslands, fresh water, and salt water. One snake, the common European adder,[3] has managed to survive in the freezing temperatures of the Arctic Circle. An astounding adaptation for a cold-blooded reptile.

Learning how to adapt to reality, instead of expecting reality to adapt to us, is essential serpent wisdom. Sometimes adapting means pivoting, finding common ground, building bridges or treating uncomfortable situations as exercises that help us grow, by expanding our horizons and getting out of our comfort zones. Psychiatrist M. Scott Peck, famous for his bestselling book *The Road Less Traveled*, defined mental health with one word: flexibility. We must learn to be flexible and adapt.

## 132    Get a Hold of Yourself

Snakes adapts in many ways, including shedding their own skin, to grow. On average, snakes shed their skin three to six times a year. We too must shed our expectations, desires, and goals, when necessary, as well as certain aspects of our external identities and social self. We must learn to let go of the outer forms and tactics we use to interact with the world, when they're no longer working for us, and take on new external forms that help us survive and thrive.

This may feel like we're not being true to ourselves, but we actually learn more about ourselves through this process. For starters, we see we're not our skin. We're not our external forms or persona. We're what's underneath. We must shed our skin when it's constricting us, to give our sense of self underneath, room to grow and expand.

Snakes also teach us how to be formidable, when we need to be. If snakes can't lay low and blend in, they coil, hood, or rattle their tails to be perceived as a threat. Even if they're terrified on the inside. But this is a last resort. Snakes aren't aggressive, as a rule. Their first line of defense is to get away. They aren't looking for a fight. They rarely have to fight because their presence alone is usually enough to let others know they shouldn't be taken lightly or treated carelessly. Serpent wisdom teaches us to develop a certain amount of fierceness that lets others know we deserve respect; we have boundaries and we're not to be mistreated.

To do this, we can learn from people who embody strength and confidence in a variety of ways. Maybe we sign up for a martial arts class or hire a personal fitness trainer. Perhaps we take a course on psychology to understand people and personality types better, or we enroll in a class that teaches us how to communicate more effectively and think more quickly on our feet. We might ask someone who embodies assertiveness to mentor us or invite a friend who has been successful in certain areas to give us honest feedback on what we could be working on. We can read books about self-improvement or listen to podcasts about developing boundaries, self-respect, and personal growth. There are many ways to learn from the worldly-wise.

Sometimes Christians are taught to be weak, as if weakness is a virtue. Some of us have been taught to be as harmless as doormats, that others can walk over. This isn't what Jesus teaches or models. Meekness in the Bible doesn't mean being weak or timid. It means to display the right blend of strength and reserve. To avoid unnecessary harshness when using strength. It's the ability to regulate your emotions, to demonstrate power and restraint at the same time. You must own your strength and power to be meek.

Some Christians misinterpret Jesus' instruction to turn the other cheek to mean we should take whatever people throw at us. Unfortunately, this kind of imbalanced teaching often comes from religious leaders who want their followers to be pushovers, who can be controlled and manipulated. These religious leaders want their followers to be docile doves, so they can be tamed, controlled, and used for their own purposes and pocketbooks. This timid nature of doves is why magicians use them in tricks. They can train doves to stay crammed up their sleeves or in tight spaces, even though this is uncomfortable or even harmful to the dove. This doesn't work with snakes though. You won't be able to shove a snake up your sleeve and make it uncomfortable for long. Snakes have boundaries and they will let you know when you cross them.

Learning to respond appropriately to those who pose a threat or cross our boundaries is critical serpent wisdom. This might mean finding our voice and the courage to speak up

## 134 Get a Hold of Yourself

for ourselves, if someone is routinely undermining or taking advantage of us. It might mean having some good questions and retorts stored in your memory to use in such situations. There are many worldly-wise sources that can help us develop boundaries and learn how to enforce them.

Yet many of us need to develop restraint in addition to boundaries. To stop looking for fights everywhere we go. Stop flying off the handle over every comment, constantly overreacting, rattling our tails or showing our fangs every time we get uncomfortable. If we're constantly escalating, people won't take us or our boundaries seriously. Or they'll avoid us. Including the people we want meaningful relationships with.

Serpent wisdom is ultimately about understanding how to thrive without engaging in battles. The goal of developing worldly wisdom is to avoid conflict and fights, when possible. To learn more effective ways of interacting with others. Not that we shy away from conflict when we need to stand up to people. But that's a last resort. Most battles are not worth the risk. Most battles leave both sides injured. Worldly wisdom helps us find creative "win-win" solutions.

Yet there are times we need to stand up for ourselves or defend others. To do this effectively we must develop enough tools, techniques, and inner strength to deal with these situations when they arise. This aspect of serpent wisdom might be best described as self-confidence, which isn't about being harsh, scrappy, or aggressive. Self-confidence is about being calm, cool, and collected.

An interesting study entitled "Attracting Assault" was conducted by Betty Grayson and Morris I. Stein to understand why criminals choose to target certain people and avoid others.[4] They recorded sixty random strangers walking along a street in New York City, then showed the video to a group of convicted offenders whose crimes included violence. The researchers asked them to select the individuals they would likely target and which ones they'd avoid. The researchers re-examined the results with another group of criminals, who confirmed the choices the original group made.

The most common trait the offenders said they'd avoid was appearing organized and "together." They avoided people who appeared composed, in control of themselves, who walked upright, in a natural manner, with a proportional stride-length and fluid motion.

The people they identified as targets had an inconsistent and dissonant quality, like they were out of harmony with themselves. The study concluded that potential targets "might be exuding vulnerability to criminals through their posture, gestures, and exaggerated movements."[5]

The point of this study is not to justify the predatory behavior of criminals or blame victims for what happens to them. Obviously. However, it reveals there are things we can develop in ourselves that let criminals, manipulators, and abusers know we're not an easy mark. (This is true in churches as well as out in the world.) We're not worth their time. We're going to be more trouble than we're worth. We will stand up for ourselves. We communicate this by being in harmony with ourselves, respecting ourselves, and having a healthy ego. However, a healthy ego is not a "big" ego or an arrogant persona, it's being comfortable and confident in who we are.

Confidence is knowing we can depend on ourselves. Confidence comes from the Latin word *confidere*, which means "to have full trust." Self-confidence is to have full trust in your self. To know you can rely on yourself. We develop self-confidence

*136* **Get a Hold of Yourself**

by keeping promises to ourselves. When we say we're going to do something, we do it. When we do what we've committed ourselves to, we learn we can trust ourselves. By contrast, when we repeatedly don't follow through on our commitments, we teach ourselves we can't depend on ourselves.

One of the best ways to build self-confidence is to set goals and follow through. Start with small goals. Cleaning our desk at work. Organizing our desktop screen on our computer. Going for a thirty-minute walk every day, or finding other ways to be active. Set goals then follow through. The more we get in the habit of attaining our goals, even small ones, the more we learn we can rely on ourselves.

Self-confidence is connected to integrity, which is knowing I am who I say I am, and I do what I say I will do. When we don't live with integrity, we lose confidence in ourselves. We don't like ourselves, which causes us to be in disharmony with ourselves, causing us to suffer in all kinds of ways. Including potentially facing unwanted attention from the predatory snakes and criminals out there. To be clear, experiencing predatory behavior is *not* the fault of the person being preyed on. But self-confidence can help us avoid many snares.

Self-confidence isn't comparative. It isn't thinking we're better or worse than others. It's knowing what we're capable of and working to expand what we're capable of. Confident people are willing to take risks and fail, because their self-worth isn't determined by failure or rejection. They know they'll learn from their mistakes and get back up again. They'll get through failure, because they've done so in the past. Yet people who are confident and wise are also humble. They ask for help when they need it. In fact, they are keener to ask for help than most people, because their self-concept isn't diminished by their need for help. We all need help sometimes. Sometimes we can't get back up on our own. We need the support and assistance of others. We need community in our lives.

We can learn much from worldly-wise people, and we must, to integrate both our serpent side and our dove side, as Jesus counsels. I have highlighted a few of the ways we can learn from snakes and worldly-wise people, while acknowledging Jesus may have had other things in mind. From a psychological perspective, however, we must develop healthy egos to thrive as competent, confident, and effective individuals in the world. I'm calling this process our serpent journey.

Yet as important as this serpent journey is, it's not the end of our growth journeys. Serpent wisdom is insufficient and incomplete. If we don't take our dove journeys, we'll stay immature. Or worse, we might become one of the venomous vipers the Bible warns us about.

## WHEN THE SERPENT BECOMES AN IDOL

The story of the bronze serpent continues in the Bible (2 Kings 18:1–4). Centuries later, the bronze serpent is still around. The Israelites kept it. They even gave it a name. Nehushtan. They were worshiping it and making offerings to it, as if it were a god. Eventually God told King Hezekiah to destroy it.

This can happen to us as well. In our personal development, we can become attached to and dependent on the savvy way of the serpent. It's helped us become clever, confident, and discerning. It's helped us find success in this snake-filled world. Consequently, we start to trust in the wisdom and ways of the serpent, more than we trust God, because it's helped us become confident, capable, and courageous. Serpent wisdom has helped us get the job we wanted, the raise we requested, the client we targeted, the partner we desired, and the possessions we coveted, because it helped us become more assertive, disciplined, and confident.

As we successfully learn from the effective, clever, and accomplished people we meet, or their books or podcasts, we learn to continually shed our skin, raise our standards, discipline ourselves to expand our capabilities, take risks, and go for what we want. As we grow and feel better about ourselves, we naturally assume the way of the serpent has all the answers. It becomes our idol. Our god. It's what we look to for guidance. But at some point, we need to smash our serpent idol, if we want to continue growing.

Once we've learned what we need from the serpent, the Spirit invites us to learn the way of the dove. The Spirit eventually invites us to take our second journey, the dove journey. Because Jesus doesn't call us to be snakes, he calls us to be serpent-doves.

# 8

# SELF

I arrived at my Airbnb rental at 8 p.m. I entered the code to open the door and was startled to see someone lounging on the sofa a few feet in front of me. Not as startled as he was to see me though. He bolted up, took an aggressive posture and in an agitated voice shouted, "Who are you? Identify yourself!"

It took me a moment to process his demand. The last time I was asked to identify myself, I showed the security officer my passport. As I contemplated the question, "Who are you?" I thought about sharing my name, marital status, occupation, and the like. However, none of that seemed relevant in the moment. Finally, I said, "I'm the person who rented this Airbnb! Who are you?" (The situation was quickly resolved when we contacted the Airbnb host. They'd mistakenly given me access to the wrong room, so they sent me the door code to my room on the other side of the building, which was uninhabited, thankfully.)

There are hundreds, if not thousands, of ways we could answer the question, "Who are you?" It's a more complicated question than it seems on the surface. It becomes even more daunting when you add the phrase "Identify yourself."

## 140 Get a Hold of Yourself

Philosophers have been trying to answer the question, "What is your 'self'?" for thousands of years. It's surprisingly difficult. My favorite definition comes from the nineteenth-century philosopher Søren Kierkegaard: "The self is a relation that relates itself to itself or is the relation's relating itself to itself in the relation; the self is not the relation but is the relation's relating itself to itself."[1] As convoluted as this definition is, Kierkegaard is right. Each of us is a complex and fluid flow of relating activity.

Another famous saying, attributed to the pre-Socratic Greek philosopher Heraclitus, states, "No man ever steps in the same river twice, for it's not the same river and he's not the same man." In other words, the "you" that you identify as "you" changes from one moment to the next. Who you feel and perceive yourself to be fluctuates.

Some days we feel young and vibrant, other days old and fragile. In a morning meeting we might view ourselves as intelligent and articulate, then foolish and unintelligible later that afternoon. Attractive and charming at a social gathering Friday night, ugly and awkward at the gym Monday morning. Brimming with confidence with these people, insecure and anxious around those people.

It's not that we become different people, obviously, but we manifest so many different variations of our "self" it becomes confusing to know who we really are. The pursuit of understanding ourselves is elusive. That's why we take personality assessments like Myers-Briggs, the Enneagram, or the Big Five personality test. We take quizzes on social media to see what Game of Thrones or Star Wars character we resemble. We see a therapist to help us figure ourselves out. We read books on self-improvement and self-discovery. The quest to understand who we are and how to be authentic can feel endless, and futile, at times.

**Self** *141*

The conundrum of identity is that we're in a constant state of flux, perpetually transforming and unfolding, yet we have a central sense of continuity to our identity as well. We change and shift, but we know we're still us. Ultimately, the "self" is a paradox. It's a shapeshifting entity that's both changing and constant. Always the same yet slightly different each moment.

Western psychology tends to approach the psyche (the sum of one's entire psychological makeup) as a multifaceted entity, with different parts, aspects, and dynamics. Sigmund Freud asserted the human psyche contains three parts: the id, ego, and superego. Carl Jung posited the psyche is made up of the ego, persona, shadow, collective unconscious, anime / animus, archetypes, and the Self. Eric Berne named the three parts of the psyche as the parent ego, the adult ego, and the child ego.

Most psychological frameworks for understanding ourselves reference the ego. A great deal of contemporary pop psychology, self-improvement writing, and spiritual literature refers to the ego as something we must transcend, dissolve, or shed. This idea comes from certain Eastern philosophies and traditions. I refer to this understanding of the ego as the "ego mind." Ego mind is the default tendency of our mind to identify with temporal aspects of our beings, like our physical appearance, strength, or accomplishments. This understanding of the ego mind is very different than the meaning of the term *ego* in Western psychology.

In Jungian psychology, the ego is the center of our field of consciousness. It's what holds our awareness of existing, and our sense of personal identity. In this context, trying to develop or maintain a healthy psyche by eliminating your ego would be like trying to get physically fit by eliminating your heart or lungs. In a word, counterproductive. The ego isn't something negative or illusory, it's a necessary part of your

## 142   Get a Hold of Yourself

psyche. Your ego is essentially who you relate to as "you" in the moment.

The problem is not that we have an ego, the problem is what our ego mind identifies with. The ego mind tends to base our identity on the past, usually focusing on negative experiences that caused us pain, fear, anxiety, and trauma. Like the time you wet the bed at a sleepover and the other kids laughed at you. Or when your best friend betrayed you and started dating the person you really liked. When your fiancé broke it off because they realized you weren't the right one for them. When your boss gave someone else the promotion you asked for and told you that you weren't manager material. These experiences stay with us and provide the basis of what our ego mind identifies with.

Negatives grab the attention of ego mind more than positives. For example, say you go to a party and nine people compliment your new hairdo, but one person says, "To be honest, that haircut doesn't work on your round face." If you're like most people, the impact of the one negative comment will significantly outweigh the nine compliments. That's what our ego minds do. It's what they're designed to do. They constantly learn from the negatives so they can figure out how to prevent us from having to live those negative experiences again in the future.

We've talked about how the first stage of our serpent journeys is about learning from all our negative experiences to protect ourselves from potential "snakebites." Anything that poses a threat to our survival, security, and confidence, like a mean comment, disrespectful act, attempt to steal our significant other, or potential scam.

However, an effective serpent journey takes us beyond identifying with the negative experiences of our past. A

**Self** *143*

healthy ego learns from the negatives while identifying with the positives. We learn to find our identity in our strengths, success, and accomplishments. Everything that reinforces our confidence that we can rely on ourselves and take care of ourselves. This is why many of us identify with our physical abilities, appearance, intellect, athletic accomplishments, degrees, titles, wealth, influence, and the like. They distinguish us from others and assure us we have what it takes to survive and thrive.

Like when you charmed your way into that exclusive club. Or when you finally beat your in-laws at Scrabble. Or when you landed a job at the firm you were hoping to work at. These are the kinds of experiences that assure us we can rely on ourselves to survive and thrive. A healthy ego learns from the negatives but finds our identity in the positives. This is the final objective of the serpent journey. To be worldly-wise, confident and capable, and feel good about who we are.

However, as we age, we recognize all these positive things are temporal. We could lose our ability to charm our way through the world, our impressive mental prowess, and our dream job. We could lose it all. Then who would we be?

Years ago, I was having a conversation about identity with my spiritual director. He asked me a curious question: "What would you have to lose for you to stop being you?"

After some reflection, I couldn't think of anything. I told him if I lost my legs, friends, titles, roles, loved ones, accomplishments, citizenship, abilities, job, even my faith, I'd still be me. I'd be profoundly impacted by all these losses—but I'd still exist as me.

He said, "Very good. Now let me push you further. What would you have to lose to stop knowing you were you. To stop experiencing you as you?"

It was a profound question. I eventually saw the answer was just one thing. Consciousness. My awareness. The only thing I could lose that would make me stop being aware that I am me—is my awareness of being me.

The dove journey is about awareness. The first stage is to identify with our awareness.

## THE DOVE JOURNEY

When Jesus says we must be pure as doves in Matthew 10:16, the Greek word used is *akeraios*, which means unmixed, simple, pure. *Akeraios* was used to describe pure wine that was not watered down, or pure gold that was not mixed with other metals. To be pure as doves is to be grounded in our essential self, which isn't tainted or diluted with anything external.

Unlike your ego mind, your essential self does not identify with your archive of positive and negative experiences, the parts within you that have been shaped and influenced by external events and other people. Your essential self is the you that is aware of these other parts within you.

For example, your essential self doesn't identify with the part of you that felt rejected by your parent, or was spurned by your love interest, or humiliated by a bully. Your essential self is the you that is *aware* of the part of you that feels and lives with this sense of rejection or humiliation. Your essential self doesn't identity with the positives either, such as your identification as the smartest, strongest, or most attractive person in the room. It's the you that's aware of this part of you that identifies with being the smartest, strongest, or most attractive person in the room.

In short, your essential self is the you that is aware of the ego mind doing its thing.

Our dove journey is about accessing and living from our essential self, which is grounded in our awareness that who we are is beyond all the things that our ego mind identifies with. The things that differentiate us from others, such as our age, gender, ethnicity, genetics, experiences, failures, and success. This, I believe, is why Paul says in Christ there is "neither Jew nor Greek, slave nor free, male nor female, for you are all one" (Galatians 3:28, my paraphrase). There is an essential self underneath our ego-differentiated identity that's in a state of "at-one-ment" with God and others.

The dove journey has two parts. First, becoming aware that we are not what we think we are. The second is becoming one in Christ, which we'll talk about in the next chapter. For now, I want to focus on the first part: We are not what we think we are.

## BECOMING AWARE OF THE EGO MIND

Ego mind interprets the present through the lens of the past. For instance, if a friend doesn't respond to our text, our ego mind searches the archives of our experiences to find a similar experience, to interpret how we should think, feel, and respond to this. It might recall the time a friend ghosted us, or when a group of friends ignored our texts when they went to a concert and didn't include us. As our ego mind recalls these events, it associates them with what we're experiencing now, and it begins to respond to the current situation as if we're reliving these archived memories. This means we're often not responding to our current reality; we're responding to our sense of fear or rejection that's rooted in our past.

When we later find out our friend had misplaced his phone and texted us as soon as he found it, we feel relieved and silly

146   **Get a Hold of Yourself**

for getting so worked up. But we'll do this again. And again, if we continue to live from our ego mind. Because our ego mind is always looking for trouble. It's always on the hunt for problems, threats, and snakes that might bite us. That's its job.

Unlike the ego mind, the essential self doesn't attach labels to what we're aware of. It doesn't associate what's happening now with the past. It doesn't assume what's happening is bad or good. Let's say someone mocks you. Your essential self isn't bothered by this or afraid of this. It's simply aware of it. However, your ego mind will be disturbed by this. It will go back into the archive of your past experiences and compare this to all the other times you've been mocked or humiliated. It will usually find the worst-case scenario. Then it begins to relive and experience the pain and alienation of your greatest humiliation, instead of processing the present moment for what it is.

The goal of the dove journey is not to stop the ego mind from doing this. That's an impossible task. The goal of the dove journey is to stay grounded in our essential self and be aware of what's unfolding, without judgment. This includes being aware of our ego mind getting bothered and overreacting. It accepts the dance of the ego mind as one more thing that's happening in the moment.

The essential self doesn't judge the ego mind doing its thing, but it doesn't get lost in it either. It continues to stay aware. Aware that we have an ego mind that does ego mind things. If we practice this long enough, we'll begin to chuckle when the ego mind starts dancing.

## BECOMING AWARE YOU'RE LOST IN THE MOVIE

Years ago, I was in a movie theater watching a movie about a man's harrowing journey of surviving in the jungle. It was an intense and captivating movie. I became caught up in the story. I was there, in the jungle. Then someone sneezed loudly in the theater. Suddenly I was aware I was in a theater, not in a jungle. I became aware of the screen, the ceiling, the dimly lit aisles, the rows of seats, and people around me eating popcorn. I zoomed out from the movie and was now having a totally different experience from a few moments earlier, when I'd been lost in the jungle.

Years later I read *The Untethered Soul* by Michael A. Singer, who used this very movie theater scenario as an analogy to distinguish the ego mind from the essential self (although he uses different terminology).

Our ego mind is the one who gets lost in the movie, in the drama of the moment. Our essential self is the one aware that we are watching a movie. Aware of the whole theater. For example, if someone condescends to us, our ego mind gets lost in the drama of this perceived disrespect. Our essential self is the one aware that the movie is just a movie, and is aware of our ego mind getting lost in the movie.

Our tendency is to get lost in the drama of life. When we do, we lose our groundedness in our essential self. We identify with our ego mind in the jungle. We return to our essential self by becoming aware we're in the theater, aware of our ego mind getting lost in the movie. To do this, we can ask ourselves a series of questions. If I'm feeling humiliated, for example, I can ask "What part of me is being humiliated?"

This question is like the loud sneeze in the movie theater. It helps me become aware that I'm watching a movie. It creates a gap in my identification with my ego mind, the part of me that is caught up in the drama, labeling this experience as bad, wrong, unfair, or in this case, humiliating.

Then I ask a follow-up question. "Who is aware of this part of me that feels humiliated?" This helps me identify with my

*148*  **Get a Hold of Yourself**

awareness and become grounded in my essential self. I'm no longer lost in the drama. I'm the one who's aware of my ego mind watching the movie.

When we live in our ego mind, our joy, peace, and content-ment are dependent on two things that we have no control over: our external reality and our past experiences (because our interpretation of our current reality is always being inter-preted through the lens of our past experiences). When we live in awareness as our essential self, we're not dependent on our external reality or the lens of our past to find peace, joy, or contentment. We can see that peace, joy, and contentment are always available to us in the present moment.

## CHOOSE YOUR FREQUENCY

In the olden days, we didn't stream our music, we listened to music on something called the radio. As far as I know, most vehicles still have radio receivers in them. Right now, there are thousands, probably millions, of songs being broadcast through the air around the planet. If you turn on a radio receiver, you'll hear a song that you couldn't hear before. It was already playing, but you couldn't hear it until you turned the radio receiver on.

If you change the frequency of the tuner to a different radio station, you'll hear a different song. As you keep changing the frequency of the tuner, tuning in to different radio stations, you'll continue to hear more songs. These songs don't start playing as soon as you tune in to them. They were already playing, but you had to turn on the radio receiver and tune in to the right frequency to hear them.

It's the same with joy, peace, and contentment. They're already being broadcast in the present moment. They're always available to you, wherever you are. But you must tune in to the right frequency to receive them.

Your ego mind is constantly changing frequencies and tuning in to different radio stations, depending on what's happening. If we lose our job it might tune in to the worry or despair frequency. If someone cuts us off on the highway, it might tune in to the anger frequency. But our essential self is always tuned in to the radio station of peace, joy, and contentment, no matter what's going on. Those frequencies are the natural resonant frequencies of the essential self. But you must tune in to awareness, to hear those "songs" being broadcast.

## RESISTANCE

You don't tune in to awareness, your essential self, by resisting the dance of the ego mind. When the ego mind is tuned in to anger, for example, you don't try to force your ego mind to stop being angry. You simply become aware that your ego mind is tuned in to anger. You notice your ego mind thinking, "This is unfair! They shouldn't have said that or done that. This is awful. I must be angry. I must be upset." The essential self doesn't engage the conversation and say, "That's not true, you shouldn't see things that way." The essential self doesn't engage the dance of the ego mind at all. It simply *notices* it.

The essential self observes the ego mind doing what it does. Without judgment. But it doesn't get lost in it. That's the only "trick" of the essential self. It's aware that we're being aware. When we do this, we're grounded in our essential self, which is always tuned in to the frequency of love, joy, peace, and contentment. This is the only way to live as our authentic self.

It's difficult, if not impossible, to be our authentic self in an ego state of mind. Our ego mind is a fickle creature,

*150* **Get a Hold of Yourself**

tossed to and fro by the waves of our distorted interpretations and responses to reality. Ego mind allows external factors and influences, filtered through the interpretive lens of our past, to determine who we are in the present. In this state, we aren't being our authentic self, we're reacting to our skewed interpretations. We aren't pure wine, we're tainted by external factors. We're not pure gold, we're mixed with other elements.

## AUTHENTIC SELF

Your authentic self is like a beautiful stained glass window. The size, shape, and material of your authentic self is determined at birth. These are the natural qualities, traits, gifts, abilities, limitations, characteristics, and personality you were born with. Over time, this stained glass window is modified, colored, and filled in by your experiences and choices. It isn't static, it changes over time, as you take your serpent and dove journeys. You continue to add nuance and detail to the complex mosaic of your authentic self as you learn, grow, and realize your potential.

However, the unique stained glass window of your authentic self remains hidden until it's illuminated. You can't see a stained glass window in the dark. It's only revealed when light shines through it. Your essential self is the divine light within you. Your stained glass window remains hidden, without the light of your essential self shining through it.

When we identify with our ego mind, we eclipse the light of the essential self within us. We "hide our light under a bushel" instead of letting our light shine, as an old song I used to sing in Sunday school put it. When we get lost in the ego mind, when we get immersed in the movie and drama of life, we overshadow the light of our essential self.

## BACK TO RESISTANCE

The ego mind is intentionally hindering the light of our essential self from illuminating our authentic self. It has learned to hide, suppress, and resist the emergence of the essential self, because it understands its job is to protect the center of our "self." It knows our "self" got hurt in the past, so it strives to protect our "self" from being exposed, so it doesn't get hurt again. If our essential self shines its light and puts our authentic self out there, it could get hurt. It could get rejected, humiliated, taken advantage of, betrayed, and so on.

The irony is our essential self is the only "part" of us that can't be hurt, by anyone or anything. Thus the essential self isn't afraid of anything, which terrifies the ego mind. In his book *How to Be an Adult*, psychotherapist David Richo calls this the "fear of fearlessness."[2] The ego mind fears this fearlessness because it's focused on staying in control. This is what we've learned on our serpent journey. To constantly evaluate what's happening and take preventive measures against anything that's potentially negative or threatening. Ego mind is based on fear. It's constantly looking for what could go wrong. This includes resisting the essential self, because the essential self has no fear, which is dangerous to the ego mind.

Perhaps an analogy will help. There's an old Taoist story about a farmer whose horse runs away. When his neighbor hears the news he says, "Oh, that's bad." The farmer responds, "Maybe, maybe not. Who can say?" The next day the horse returns with seven other horses. The neighbor says, "That's great. You have eight horses now." The farmer responds, "Maybe, maybe not. Who can say?" The next day the farmer's son is trying to break one of the new horses, falls, and breaks his leg. The neighbor says, "Oh, that's awful." The farmer says, "Maybe, maybe not. Who can say?" The next day the

*152* **Get a Hold of Yourself**

army passes through the region and the general conscripts all the young men to go fight against their enemies. Because the farmer's son has a broken leg, he isn't conscripted. The neighbor says, "How fortunate. That's great." The farmer replies, "Maybe, maybe not. Who can say?"

The ego mind is like the neighbor, constantly judging everything as good or bad. The essential self is like the farmer, who calmly accepts whatever happens, without judgment. It's this fearless capacity of our essential self to accept "what is" (whatever is, isn't, or could be happening) that terrifies our ego mind. Because the essential self doesn't resist "what is"—even if it's bad, scary, or evil according to the ego mind. Which goes against everything the ego mind believes and stands for.

Another confounding teaching of Jesus is when he says, "Do not resist the evil" (see Matthew 5:39). The Greek word used here is *poneros*, which means bad, evil, full of labors, annoyance, hardships—all the things the ego mind most actively resists. Jesus is inviting us to shift from our ego mind resistance to essential self awareness. Essential self doesn't resist *poneros*. It's simply aware of what is happening, without judgment, while also being aware of how our ego mind is judging what's happening, and getting lost in the drama.

This isn't to say we should never deal with things that are happening or stand up to injustice or protect ourselves or our loved ones. We should. But if we want to be free to respond most effectively to the ebb and flow of life, with love, peace, joy, and wisdom, we must do it from a place of being grounded in our fearless and nonjudgmental essential self, rather than getting lost in our fearful and judgmental ego mind.

In Victor Hugo's novel *Les Misérables*, Jean Valjean spends nineteen years in prison for stealing a loaf of bread. After he is released, he knocks on the local bishop's door and asks for a place to sleep for the night. The bishop gives him a warm meal and a bed to sleep in. After the bishop is asleep, Jean steals a bunch of silverware and flees. The police catch him and bring him back to the bishop's house to answer for his crime. The bishop tells the policeman Jean didn't steal the items, rather, they were a gift. Then he tells Jean to wait, because he'd forgotten the best part of his gift. The bishop returned with two large silver candlesticks and gives them to Jean.

This act of grace changes Jean's life. In fact, Jean never sells the candlesticks. He keeps them, as a symbol of the gift of grace that changed his life. The end of the book describes Jean passing away underneath the light of the candles, held in the same candlesticks the bishop had given him many years ago.

The bishop responded to Jean's crime from a place of essential self, not with his ego mind. The ego mind would get lost in the drama, judging and labeling the crime. "How dare you repay my kindness by stealing from me. You took what belongs to me. That's wrong. Once a thief always a thief. You haven't changed. You deserve to go back to prison." But the bishop doesn't resist the "evil" theft of the silverware, because his essential self was aware there was more going on than a crime. He saw this was an opportunity to change a man's life. To increase love and goodness in the world.

This isn't to say people should never face consequences for wrongdoing. The point is our ego mind will constantly miss the greater movement of God's grace, healing, and renewal in the world, because it will be focused on resisting what is evil, wrong, unfair, and unacceptable. It cannot accept "what is" without judgment because its nature is to resist a great deal of "what is" and what could be, for the sake of retaining control, protecting ourselves and what's rightfully ours. The essential

*154* **Get a Hold of Yourself**

self is aware of the bigger picture. It sees the whole theater, not just what's happening in the movie.

## WHAT ELSE IS TRUE?

When something painful, scary, or uncomfortable occurs, it grabs the full attention of our ego mind. This is our default wiring as humans. If you stub your toe or see something that looks like a snake in the grass, your ego mind puts all its attention on this, because it's a perceived threat to your survival, well-being, and happiness. When we feel rejection, failure, or an injustice, it gets the full attention of our ego mind. This is how we've learned to protect ourselves on our serpent journeys.

Say you don't get a job you really wanted because the company claimed you're not the right fit. You're upset. You were really excited about this opportunity. Your ego mind says, "This is wrong. This is unfair. They didn't even give me a chance." Your ego mind is getting lost in the movie. It has tunnel vision. This injustice is all it can see. To help find your way out and back to the awareness of your essential self, ask this important question: "What else is true?"

Don't ask if what you're thinking or feeling is true. That would be to engage the dance of the ego mind and stay lost in the movie. It doesn't really matter if it's true. Your ego mind is already lost in the drama, it can't be rational and nonjudgmental about your current reality in this state.

Ask, "What else is true?"

"Even if it's true this is unfair, it's also true that I have a lot of people who care about me and support me. It's also true that I've been working hard on developing new skills, and several people have noticed and commended me for this. It's also true the sun is shining today, and the sky is a beautiful shade of blue. It's perfect weather for a hike, to go and clear my mind. It's also true that I have tickets to a concert this weekend, that my best friend and I are looking forward to." And so on.

This question, "What else is true?," expands your awareness to see there are many things true in this moment. Your ego mind is choosing to get lost in one particular "truth," which may or may not be true. The point of this question isn't to convince your ego mind that the movie it's lost in isn't true. The point is to become aware of the full breadth of what is happening in the present moment. By zooming out from what the ego mind is focused on, you free yourself to experience the fullness of reality in the present moment, including the beauty, abundance, joy, peace, and contentment available to you in this moment.

## IDENTIFYING WITH OUR ESSENTIAL SELF

Another helpful tool to help us tune in to our essential self comes from a psychotherapy model called Internal Family Systems, or IFS. It posits the "Self" is characterized by eight qualities, known as the 8 Cs: curiosity, calm, clarity, compassion, confidence, creativity, courage, and connectedness.[3] To help our essential self emerge, we must tap into the 8 Cs.

For example, if you're feeling anxious, you might engage curiosity and ask, "Why is this part of me so anxious? What is it afraid of? What happened to it?" When you begin to feel curiosity, your essential self is emerging. As you become aware of the part of you that's anxious, you're now identifying with your essential self, the one who is aware of this part, rather than identifying with the anxious part in you.

Learning how to let my essential self emerge and live in awareness has made a huge difference in my life. I typically do this by tuning in to curiosity or compassion. Say someone cuts me off in traffic and I'm feeling angry. My ego mind is lost in this movie. To tune in to essential self, I focus on finding my curiosity or compassion. I usually begin by pausing, taking a few deep breaths, and asking, "Is there any part of me that's curious about why I'm so angry? Is there any part of me that feels compassion towards the person who cut me off?" Most of the time I'm able to tap into curiosity or compassion. When I do, my entire state changes. I feel lighter, grounded, and whole. I see the entire situation, including the person who cut me off, differently.

Like anything, this gets easier the more we do it. I'm not saying this always works for me, or that it always happens quickly. But the more I practice this, the results are astounding. My experience of the same moment is completely transformed, sometimes drastically, in the blink of an eye. I can be completely frustrated one minute, and have a heart filled with joy and peace a few seconds later, as my essential self emerges and transforms how "I" see the situation.

Most of the time I don't live with my essential self as my center. My ego mind is usually at the center and in control of my consciousness, constantly shifting and merging with the various parts within me. My sense of "I" is constantly changing as it temporarily merges or identifies with one part, then another part, and so on.

For example, one minute "I" might be identified with my inner perfectionist, attempting to do my best on a project at work. A few minutes later, my "I" merges with my inner critic, pointing out my lack of progress. Then my boss walks into my office and "I" quickly transition into my professional self. During my commute home, I'm exhausted and remember

**Self** *157*

something unfair that happened earlier. Now "I" am my wounded inner child, sulking because everything is unfair.

Who "I" am in the moment depends on which part, role, or perspective my ego mind has merged with, or become lost in, in that moment. When this merging happens, my sense of self temporarily fuses with that part. I see, feel, and engage with the world as if that part is "me." The way I let my essential self emerge and become my center is to become aware that I'm the one being aware of my ego mind doing its thing. One of the best ways to do this is to tap into one of the 8 C's: curiosity, calm, clarity, compassion, confidence, creativity, courage, or connectedness.

As we journey from learning from snakes to learning from doves, we learn to become aware of the ego mind and tune in to the essential self. The first task of this dove journey is to let awareness, our essential self, emerge and become the center of our consciousness. To realize we're not who we think or feel we are. We're not even the thinker or feeler. We're the one who is aware of the thinker and feeler, namely, the ego mind.

As we practice this, we realize what Paul meant when he said it's no longer he who lives, but Christ who lives in him. Here's a reinterpretation of Galatians 2:20 for the dove journey: "It's no longer my ego mind that I identity with and let live my life, it is 'Christ in me' that is my true identity, and lives my life." Becoming aware of "Christ in us" is the second part of the dove journey.

9

# CHRIST

When Tammy and I were looking to buy a minivan to accommodate our growing family, we looked at some used Toyota Siennas. They had great reviews and a few of our friends owned them and loved them. As we began searching for the best Sienna at the best price, a curious thing happened. We noticed them everywhere. Every other vehicle on the road seemed to be a Toyota Sienna. How had we never noticed this before?

There's a name for this. It's called the Baader-Meinhof phenomenon, or the frequency illusion. When you learn something new or are focused on something new, your mind starts noticing it everywhere, making it seem more common than it actually is.

## FOCUS MATTERS

Let's try a little experiment. (Only do this if you're in a situation where you're able to take a break and close your eyes.)

Set a timer for seven seconds. Start the timer and look around. Notice everything in the room that's green. Find as many things as you can that are green.

[Stop, here, and try the experiment. Then return to the text.]

*159*

*160*  **Get a Hold of Yourself**

Now that the timer's up, read the next sentence and follow its instructions.

Close your eyes and name five things in the room that are red.

Most people can't. They can name plenty of things that are green, but they can't name anything, or only a few things, that are red.

In life, we notice what we're looking for and overlook everything else. In Matthew 7:7–8 Jesus essentially says that the things we find are the things we're looking for, the answers we receive are based on the questions we're asking, and the doors that are opened to us are the ones we're knocking on. What we focus on matters. It determines our experience of reality. This means what we see in others, the world, and ourselves is not an accurate picture, because it's never the whole picture. It's based on what we're focused on.

Our ego minds look for two things most tenaciously:

Evidence that supports what we already believe.

Problems and potential snakebites.

As you become aware of your ego mind at work, you'll notice it's an elite problem finder. There's no end to the trouble it can find. When Jesus says, "In this world you will have trouble" (John 16:33), he's saying there will always be problems, hardship, and pain. You can't escape them, because your ego mind will find them. But these problems and issues don't have to determine your experience of reality or quality of life.

Jesus says when we're spiritually awakened, we become aware of a hidden reality called the kingdom of God. What I call the Divine Reality. You start to notice what's right with the world. You begin to "taste and see that God is good" and discover "those who seek the LORD lack no good thing" (see

Psalm 34:8–10). You "see the goodness of the LORD in the land of the living" (Psalm 27:13). You don't have to wait for the afterlife to experience God's goodness. It becomes your reality here and now. You see how much beauty, love, peace, and joy there is in each moment, because that's what you're looking for. And now you have "eyes to see and ears to hear."

When your consciousness is aware of God with you and within you, your eyes are opened to see the abundance of the fruit of the Spirit: love, joy, peace, goodness, and the like. You see they are always here, always available in the present moment. Because your focus is no longer divided between your ego mind and your essential self. Your eye, your focus, is single.

Jesus says, "Your eye is the lamp of your body. If your eye is single, your whole being is healthy and full of light" (see Matthew 6:22). When you see through the single lens of essential self awareness, your whole being is healthy and full of light. When you stop identifying with and seeing through the varied parts, thoughts, and feelings that your ego mind gets lost in, you see God's light all around you and within you. You're aware of, and begin to live in, the Divine Reality. This is the second task of the dove journey. To be spiritually awakened to the Divine Reality within us. What Paul calls "Christ in us."

## SPIRIT BAPTISM

The serpent is a symbol of the fall of humanity in the Garden of Eden. The serpent opens our eyes to dualistic thinking, to see there's both good and evil in the world. This is an important part of our psychological development. However, this lens is insufficient if we want to be free to be our authentic self, and love God and others, as we love ourselves.

*162* **Get a Hold of Yourself**

After a successful serpent journey, Jesus invites us to take our dove journey. The dove is a symbol of the Holy Spirit. To become dove-like is to become Spirit-like. Our dove journey culminates with a spiritual awakening Jesus calls the baptism of the Holy Spirit.

It's important to note that Jesus is introduced as the Messiah the same way in all four gospels. This might not sound note-worthy, but it's exceedingly rare for all four gospels to recount the same event, let alone the same way. Only four events before the final week of Jesus' life are recorded in all four gospels:

1. The ministry of John the Baptist
2. John's announcement that Jesus is the Messiah
3. Jesus starting his ministry in Galilee
4. The miracle of Jesus feeding the five thousand

That's it. Not even Jesus' birth is recounted in all four gospels. Yet they all record John introducing Jesus as the Messiah, with the exact same job description. He is introduced as the one who will "baptize people with the Holy Spirit" (Matthew 3:11; Mark 1:7–8; Luke 3:16; John 1:26–27, 30–34).

In the book of Acts, the risen Jesus tells his disciples not to go anywhere or do anything, until they've received the baptism of the Holy Spirit (Acts 1:4–5). They can't be the church, the body of Christ, without this. The birth of the church happens at Pentecost. Likewise, our spiritual rebirth as individuals occurs when we're baptized with the Spirit.

The Greek word for baptize is *baptizo*, which means to merge. To be baptized in the Spirit is to have our consciousness, our awareness, merged with the Spirit. It's having our awareness immersed in Divine Presence.

One of the oldest documented uses of the Greek word *baptizo* outside the Bible is an ancient pickling recipe. Spirit baptism is like being pickled in the Spirit. Although this sounds silly, it evokes a visual that offers a helpful perspective. In Spirit baptism, our consciousness is soaked in the presence of the Holy Spirit so that our being takes on the flavor of the divine. Like an egg pickled in vinegar, our awareness is saturated with the Spirit, transforming who and what we manifest in the world.

Now there's still a sense of separateness in this pickled union. When you taste a pickled egg, it tastes both like an egg and the vinegar it's been pickled in. For me to be baptized with the Spirit is to be a divine-flavored Troy. I'm still Troy, but a Spirit-saturated Troy. Like a pickled egg is still an egg, but a different kind of egg.

## THE ONENESS OF BEING IN CHRIST

The title *Christ* signifies the merging of humanity and divinity in the same person. Jesus is the "Christ" because he's the one in whom humanity and divinity have merged. When Paul uses the phrase "Christ in you" he's referring to this same reality occurring within us. "Christ in you" is your human spirit merged with God's Spirit. Divinity and humanity coexisting, as one, in your being.

Jesus elaborates on this idea, saying, "I am the vine, and you are the branches. The one who abides in me, and I in him, will bear much fruit" (see John 15:5). The reality of abiding "in Christ" resembles the way a branch is one with a vine. The branch is one with the vine, but it's also distinct from the trunk. The life and growth of each branch, however, is dependent on the divine "sap" flowing from the trunk of the vine. This sap only flows into a branch that is merged with the vine. Likewise, Divine Presence only flows into our consciousness when it's merged or in a state of "at-one-ment" with the Spirit.

164 **Get a Hold of Yourself**

Our essential self is not God. It's one with God. There's a big difference between being God and being one with God. Your essential self is not God. It's the "you" that's aware of your oneness with God.

Paul refers to this merging of humanity and divinity within us as "Christ in you." He sums up the entirety of the mystery of the gospel with this phrase, "Christ in you" (Colossians 1:25–27). He says this is the central truth of the gospel that has been kept hidden for ages. It remains hidden in many churches today. To experience "Christ in you" is to become aware that the same Spirit that lived in Jesus, and raised Jesus from the dead, abides in you (Romans 8:11).

## DEATH AND REBIRTH

How do we experience Spirit baptism? How do we become aware of "Christ in us"? We must experience a death to self and rebirth. This means, in part, we must stop identifying with our ego mind and be grounded in our essential self.

When Paul says, "It's no longer I who live, but Christ who lives in me" (Galatians 2:20), he's not saying Paul, the human being, has ceased to exist. Obviously. He's saying he no longer identifies with his ego mind. He understands his authentic self is not based on all the positive and negative things his ego mind identifies with, that distinguish him from God and other people. He's become aware that his true identity is his awareness of the image of God within him. His true identity is Christ (the merging of God and humanity) in his own being. This is what Jesus was referring to when he said the Divine Reality, the kingdom of God, is within you (see Luke 17:21).

To be baptized in the Spirit is to be aware of the Spirit of Christ within you. That your oneness with God is who you really are.

## TO SEE GOD EVERYWHERE

Jesus says, "No one can see and live in the Divine Reality unless they are born a second time" (see John 3:3). To be reborn requires a death to self. Our death to self happens when we stop identifying with our ego mind. Our rebirth occurs when we're awakened to the reality of our essential self, our awareness that we are one with God.

The good news is the quality of life on the other side of this death and rebirth experience exponentially surpasses the level of anguish we endure in this "letting go" process. Jesus says we tap into abundance on the other side. We plunge into an unending reservoir of infinite joy, peace, wisdom, meaning, fulfillment, and love. We become aware of the very presence of God.

My spiritual director once told me, "To see God everywhere is the sign of your spiritual birth." To be spiritually awakened is to see God in all things and in all people. The nineteenth-century English poet Elizabeth Barrett Browning put it this way: "Earth's crammed with heaven, and every common bush afire with God: But only he who sees, takes off his shoes."[1] Most of us don't take off our shoes because we're stuck in our ego mind. We don't have spiritually awakened senses to see God's presence all around us. This is why Jesus consistently says we must have "eyes to see and ears to hear."

When speaking to the religious leaders in his time, Jesus told them the Divine Reality will not come in the ways they're expecting. Those who find it don't say, "Oh, there it is" or "Look, it's over there." They see the Divine Reality is within them (see Luke 17:20–21). Seeing God everywhere begins with sensing God's Spirit within us.

Paul says, "Do you not know that you yourselves are God's temple, and that God's Spirit dwells in you?" (see

166   **Get a Hold of Yourself**

1 Corinthians 3:16). Many Christians believe this but haven't experienced it. When we become aware of this, our eyes are opened to see God everywhere, because God has saturated our consciousness. This is how you know you've been spiritually awakened. When the Spirit permeates the lens through which we see, the Spirit's presence pervades everything we see. The whole world, everyone and everything in it, is set ablaze with the light of God's presence. How could it be otherwise? God is omnipresent. The psalmist said there's no place we can go to flee God's presence (Psalm 139:7). Paul says, "In God, we live and move and have our being" (see Acts 17:28). When our eyes are opened to see the Divine Reality, we sense the omnipresence of God.

How do we receive Spirit baptism? Jesus says all we need to do is ask. Here's my interpretation of Luke 11:13: "If you people, living in your self-centered ego minds, know how to give good gifts to your children, imagine how eager your good and loving Father is to give the gift of the Holy Spirit to those who ask for this." Just ask. However, remember what you're asking for. Your spiritual birth will require a death to self.

## LIFE ON THE OTHER SIDE OF SPIRIT BAPTISM

I've had many moments of being overwhelmed by God's presence within me and all around me. When I go for hikes in beautiful nature settings, it's almost too easy. But as I walk in awareness, these moments occur when I least expect it. Like when I'm washing dishes, something I don't love to do, and I suddenly sense God in the water, in the movement of my hands, in the dim light of the sun throwing its last rays through the kitchen window at dusk. When you're tuned in, every moment reveals God's presence.

Years ago, an elder in my church rebuked me for a number of things, particularly my preaching. He was angry, lashing out, and attacking me with a strange intensity. He called me a fool. As he continued his rant, my blood began to boil. My Scottish rage wanted to strike back. Instead, I did something I'd learned called "practicing the presence." I focused on being aware of God's presence in the room, in the situation, in the elder with me. As I opened my heart and mind to the Holy Spirit, I felt an incredible wave of love for this elder. It surprised me. I could barely contain it. I wanted to embrace him as my brother. I didn't. I just listened, attentively. When he was done, I thanked him and told him I would seriously consider what he'd shared. I meant it. Then I asked to pray with him. As I "practiced the presence" I prayed with honesty, love, and compassion. I blessed him. Afterwards, I hugged him. He said, "Thank you," and left.

When he left, my ego mind started doing its thing. It wanted to defend myself against his accusations. It wanted to attack him and discount what he said. It started judging and labeling him as the real fool in this situation. As I was aware of my ego mind dancing, I focused on staying grounded in my awareness of my oneness with God. Then the Spirt brought a passage to mind I'd read a few days earlier. Proverbs 12:1: "Whoever loves discipline loves knowledge, but whoever hates correction is stupid." I literally laughed out loud. God had just called my ego mind stupid!

It doesn't matter whether we feel the correction we receive is warranted or not. The essential self doesn't resist it. Wisdom is open to learning from it. As I prayerfully reflected with the Spirit, I learned from this man's feedback. He made a few good points. Sometimes I'm too radical and theological in my preaching, for example.

*168* **Get a Hold of Yourself**

I also realized my ego mind's perception that this elder was attacking me wasn't real. This movie was only real if I identified with my ego mind. My essential self recognized something else was happening. I was being offered a pile of wheat and chaff. A wise person who hungers after truth will gather the wheat and discard the chaff. They don't get offended by the chaff, they're grateful for the wheat.

To put it another way, if you're eating a peach and bite into the pit, it doesn't make sense to get upset with the peach. It comes with a pit. There's nothing to get upset about. Just don't eat the pit. It would be ridiculous to think a banana was trying to offend you by having a peel. Bananas have peels. It's not a personal affront. Just peel the banana, throw the peel away, and eat the banana.

When correction and discipline come our way, don't get upset with the pits and peels they often come with. "Yeah, but he called me a fool. That's disrespectful. He can't talk to me that way. . ." Okay, don't eat that part. Separate the wheat from the chaff and move on. Take the things worth receiving in the correction and toss the rest. When we get defensive and resist the whole fruit of reproof, because it has a peel or a pit, we're being stupid. That's God's word, not mine.

One of the greatest insights I gleaned from this experience was seeing how much peace, joy, and contentment I experienced as I continued my conversation with God, even though this elder had called me a fool. This could have easily ruined my day. I could have been stewing in anger or resentment, or feeling insecure all day, if I had identified with my ego mind. But this experience didn't take away my peace and joy, it increased my peace and joy, because I didn't identify with the part that felt like I was being attacked and labeled a fool. I was the one aware of everything that was happening. Including my ego mind dancing, doing its thing, while God's presence was guiding, teaching, and encouraging me.

This is the quality of life available to us all the time, when we're grounded in our essential self, aware of God's presence all around us and within us.

## THE "ENOUGHNESS" OF NOW

I've met a few people who have integrated their essential self as the center from which they live and interact with the world. Most of us recognize these people when we meet them. It's as if they have figured life out. They feel at home in the present moment, in their own skin, wherever they are and whoever they're with. I suspect this is what we all long for, deep down. To be free to sing and dance like no one's watching. To not care if anyone is watching. To be free to pursue our creative interests without having to justify them as productive or good enough. To be free to release our awkward laughs, quirky sense of humor, and giddiness at the seemingly trivial and inconsequential pleasures of life. To be liberated to be okay when we're alone, unacknowledged and un-called-upon, feeling no fear, insignificance, or resentment, because we're confident in the purpose, meaning, and value of our lives. Where the need for affirmation or approval from others to feel worthy, significant, and loved fades from our lives. To be free to speak truth as a genuine act of love, rather than speaking our truth from a need to be right, noticed, or admired.

When we're grounded in essential self, we see there's always enough in the present moment. This is the power, the genius, of the essential self. It's immersed in the wholeness, oneness, and fullness of "what is," and doesn't need more. There's no perceived lack in the present moment, no matter the circumstance. The "enoughness" of the moment is enough.

*170*  **Get a Hold of Yourself**

One of the most famous passages in the Bible, Psalm 23, describes what it's like to be centered in one's essential self, walking in communion and harmony with our Creator. Here's my paraphrase of the twenty-third Psalm.

> When God is my Companion and Guide, I don't experience a desire for more. I lack nothing. I can relax and enjoy the beauty of nature and be connected to God's creation. I have no fear. There is nothing to fear, not even death, for God is with me. There's always abundance. Even if I'm surrounded by danger and enemies. Life is a bountiful feast when I walk with my Creator. My cup overflows. I live in the overflow of God's goodness and abundance. God's unconditional love surrounds me every minute of every day. For I dwell in God's presence, and I know I'll dwell in God's presence forever.

To walk in communion and harmony with our Creator is to enjoy abundance, tap into the overflow of the Divine Reality, drink from the fountain of life and be content. This enoughness of the moment might be a moment in worship, a hilarious scene, a catchy melody, the flickering flame of a campfire, a moment of grief that puts us in touch with love, a revealing disappointment, a difficult challenge that pushes us to our limits and opens new growth opportunities. There's a near infinite number of opportunities each day to be nourished by the enoughness of the present moment.

The essential self knows each moment is enough, and showing up is enough. Putting our authentic self out there is enough. Being fully present in the moment brings a surprising and amazing contentment with "what is." However, we usually only understand this after decades of playing a game we never really wanted to play in the first place. The game

**Christt** *171*

of becoming someone other than who we are—and expecting something other than "what is"—to bring us fulfillment.

To live in awareness is to live in the Divine Reality and experience the enoughness in each moment—and be satisfied. To see God's grace is enough. I am enough. This moment is enough. This is true freedom.

When we're living in the enoughness of the present moment, we have everything we need. Jesus says when you abide in the Divine Reality that abides in you (see Luke 17:21), everything else you're looking for will be added to your life (Matthew 6:33). Peace, joy, love, contentment—it's all flowing into our lives from the vine we're connected to. Right here, right now. No matter what else is happening.

Yet fully engaging the enoughness of the moment doesn't mean we deny or resist the need for change. The world needs to change. There's great injustice, suffering, and oppression in this world. We also have an innate need and desire to change ourselves. We need to grow. We want to grow. We're created for growth, and growth is change. The need and desire for change is one more part of the present moment. It's part of what makes each moment enough. We never escape the way of paradox.

To truly immerse ourselves in the enoughness of the moment is to embrace the paradoxical reality of not needing to change while needing to change. Yet when we're fully grounded in our essential self, we find the need to change is not based on some future event or outcome we must strive for, it's a present reality, already unfolding, in God's time. That we let happen—and participate in.

Like the bishop in *Les Misérables* who was aware that stealing was wrong, that crimes must be dealt with, that criminals need to change, while being aware the justice system is often

172   **Get a Hold of Yourself**

unjust and needs to change. That nineteen years in prison for stealing a loaf of bread isn't justice. Even more important, the bishop was aware of the potential to change Jean's life. Yet he was aware that going with the flow of what was happening (even though theft is wrong), rather than resisting it, was the most potent means of change. This moment of grace changed Jean and blessed far more people than if the bishop had demanded Jean change his ways and be punished for his crime.

The bishop didn't see Jean as a criminal, an enemy, or a threat to society. He saw himself in Jean. He saw the image of God in Jean. This is how we see others when we live in the Divine Reality.

## ALL GOD'S CHILDREN

One of the great hindrances to our rebirth is religion. Many believers assume they've been spiritually awakened, when the only shift they've experienced is that their ego mind has become religious or spiritually identified. Ego mind loves to identify with anything that makes us feel separate, right, special, or better than others. Ego mind loves to identify as one of the saved ones, one of the true believers, the faithful, the righteous, the enlightened, or the born again. We can be very devout, active in our church and faith, but never experience a spiritual awakening. Jesus reminds us, we can call him our Lord and Savior, do great works of faith, even cast out demons in his name, without knowing him, and without letting ourselves be known by him (see Matthew 7:21–23). To identify as a Christian or a spiritual person doesn't mean we've awakened to the Spirit of Christ within us. One of the ways we can discern if we're living in the Divine Reality is by how we see and treat others.

**Christ** *173*

If we don't view others through the lens of love, we're not walking in harmony with the Spirit. John says if we say we love God but don't love others, we are liars (see 1 John 4:20). He continues, "For whoever does not love their brother and sister, whom they have seen, cannot love God, whom they have not seen" (1 John 4:20). Our love for God and our neighbors is interconnected. Our neighbor is anyone and everyone, especially those who need our help (see Luke 10:25–37). To love God is to love everyone. To love everyone is to love God. Love is a natural expression of being aware of our "at-one-ment" with God and humanity.

To live in awareness of "Christ in us" is to know we're made in the image of God. It is to experience God looking at us and saying, "Wow! It's like looking in the mirror." When we know we're the image bearers of the Most High, we become imitators of the Most High. We're free to be fully present with others, without seeking anything in return, as God is. We're free to love and share generously, without expecting anything in return, as God does.

The way we see other people changes as our eyes adjust to life in the Divine Reality. We see we're not only one with God, we're one with all people who are made in the image of God. When we see other people, even our enemies, we realize, "Wow. It's like looking in a mirror. You're just like me. You're made in the image of God. You have an ego mind, that's doing ego mind things. You're complicated and contradictory, just like me. You are unconditionally loved by God, and you are loved by me."

Our eyes are opened to see the image of God in all human beings. We're able to glimpse the light of God in everyone. As the gospel of John says, "Through him [Christ] all things were made. . . . In him was life, and that life was the light

174 **Get a Hold of Yourself**

of all people. . . . The true light that gives light to everyone" (John 1:3–4, 9). We see the Christ light that is within us is in everyone, even though sometimes it's dim. It's hard to see it in some people. Just as it was hard to see it in ourselves for most of our lives.

When I'm caught up in my ego mind, I can be a judgmental, petty, and selfish person. When I'm grounded in my essential self, when I live in awareness of "Christ in me," I'm a different person. A new creature. I'm my authentic self. I'm overwhelmed by God's love for people. I see the image of God in them, and God's love flows through me. To live in awareness of our oneness with God is to live in a state of "at-one-ment" with God and everyone who's made in the image of God. Which is everyone. And the natural expression of this realization is love.

As wonderful as it is to live in this awakened state, the truth is I don't live this way a lot of the time. It's still a struggle. Which is the subject of the next chapter. The struggle of authenticity.

10

# AUTHENTICITY

In the tale of two wolves, a wise grandfather tells his young grandson, "There's a battle going on inside of you, inside of every person, between a good wolf and a bad wolf."

The grandson gets very concerned and asks, "Which wolf will win, grandpa?"

"The one you feed," the grandfather replies.[1]

There's an internal struggle within all of us. A battle for control. In this chapter we'll examine the struggle to be our authentic self, beginning with the struggle of embracing our contradictions.

## PETER'S PARADOX

At the Last Supper, Jesus told his disciples he would soon be arrested, and they would all abandon him. Peter flexed his plucky bravado in front of the other men, passionately pledging to never forsake Jesus, no matter what.

Jesus replied, "Peter, before the night is over, before the rooster crows tomorrow morning, you will have denied me three times."

Peter doubled down, protesting even more emphatically.

"No! Even if I must die, I'll never deny you, Jesus."

Anyone familiar with this story knows what happens. A few hours later, Peter denied knowing Jesus, three times. Then a rooster crowed, and Peter went outside and wept bitterly.[2]

This broke Peter. His self-image was shattered. Peter had always viewed himself as the courageous one. This is a consistent theme in his story. Peter boldly left his livelihood, family, and possessions to follow Jesus. He was the only disciple to step out of a fishing boat in the middle of the Sea of Galilee, in the middle of a raging storm, to attempt the impossible and walk on water with Jesus. Peter was the only one who pulled out a sword the night Jesus was arrested, to bravely resist the cohort of soldiers, even though they were vastly outnumbered and out-armed.

Although Peter was sometimes perceived as reckless, no one questioned his bravery. His courage was part of his identity. He took pride in being courageous. Yet that night, an ugly truth was revealed. Despite all his bravado, he was a coward. A coward who denied knowing his best friend, rabbi, and Messiah, because he was afraid.

Peter was confronted with the shadow of his cowardice that night. He assumed this is how everyone would see him now. For this is how he saw himself. This is why he wept bitterly that night. Not only had he lost Jesus, he'd lost his identity. He was no longer Peter the courageous. He was Peter the coward.

The truth is, Peter was both courageous and cowardly. But he didn't have the capacity to hold this paradox about himself. In Peter's mind, he was either a coward or courageous. He couldn't be both. This is how most of us view ourselves as well. We struggle to accept our paradoxical nature. Until something forces us to face our contradictions head on.

## PETER'S CAVE OF SHAME

Peter's failure to live up to his valiant promise, when tested by fire, was like an existential earthquake that cracked the surface of his fearless identity, exposing his cowardice. Although not always as extreme as Peter's fall from grace, moments like this happen to all of us. When they do, we're forced to face our gaping contradictions.

These gaps between how we want to be perceived and what's been revealed about us can engulf our consciousness. This is what happened to Peter. He spiraled downward, forced to face everything he'd denied about himself. He descended into his cave of shame, where he'd buried all the stuff he assumed made him unworthy and unlovable in the eyes of God, forced to face what he despised about himself, and accept it as part of who he was. To fully appreciate what happens next in Peter's story, we must back up a bit.

Three years earlier, Peter met Jesus on the shore of the Sea of Galilee. Peter, James, and John had returned after fishing all night, without catching a thing. Jesus told them to go back out and cast their nets one more time. Peter didn't know Jesus yet, but he knew who Jesus was. He tried to explain to Jesus the futility of his suggestion, but out of exhaustion and respect, he reluctantly agreed. When they did what Jesus suggested, they caught so many fish, their nets began to break.

This was Peter's most successful moment as a fisherman. The greatest single haul of his career. Jesus immediately called Peter to leave his fishing nets and become his apprentice. This suggests to me that success isn't always indicative of our true path and calling in life. Just because we're good at something, and God blesses us with success in it, that doesn't mean we're being true to who we are if we continue doing it. It's noteworthy Jesus invited Peter to leave his life as a fisherman, at

## 178  Get a Hold of Yourself

the pinnacle of his success as a fisherman, to become a spiritual leader.

For the next three years, Jesus taught Peter about the kingdom of God and trained him to be a spiritual leader. Then Jesus was arrested, Peter abandoned him, and Jesus was executed.

Several days later, Peter told James and John he was going fishing (see John 21). Peter wasn't just blowing off steam here. He was returning to his former life and identity. He was giving up on his potential to become the person Jesus had called him to be. In his eyes, he was no longer worthy to be a spiritual leader.

The irony is that the other disciples followed him. They followed Peter, because they still saw him as a leader, even after his cowardly act. But Peter didn't see himself as a leader anymore. He couldn't see clearly in his cave of shame. None of us can.

The Bible says Peter was stripped naked in the fishing boat that night (see John 21:7). We don't really know why. The text doesn't mention any of the other disciples being naked. It's a curious but significant detail for the gospel story to include. It's symbolic of Peter's vulnerability. He'd been exposed as a coward. His true colors were out in the open, for all to see.

Sometimes the cracks in our surface reveal to others what we're most ashamed of as well. This is perhaps our biggest fear. That our deepest shame will be exposed to the world around us. That people will see "who we really are." They'll see the ugly truth underneath the image we project to the world. It's hard to recover after this happens. It can feel hopeless. That's exactly how Peter felt.

Peter and the disciples fished all night and, once again, they didn't catch a thing. In the morning, a stranger appeared on the shore and told them to cast their net on the other side of

**Authenticity** *179*

the boat. The Bible says, "When they did, they were unable to haul the net into the boat because of the large number of fish" (John 21:6). They immediately knew the stranger was Jesus. They remembered the same thing had happened three years ago, the day Jesus had called them to leave their fishing nets and become his disciples.

As soon as Peter realized it was Jesus, he covered up. He tried to hide his nakedness, vulnerability, and shame. He tried to hide who he really was from Jesus. We often do the same thing. We try to hide from God what everyone else can see. An act of ultimate folly and futility.

When the disciples arrived on shore, Jesus cooked a few fish and loaves of bread over a fire and served them breakfast. Afterwards, he called Peter aside for a private conversation, where he asked Peter a single question, three times.

"Do you love me?"

Each time Jesus asked this question, it cut Peter more deeply. It opened the crack, the gap, even wider, pouring salt in the wound. Jesus intentionally opened this gap because it was essential for Peter to let God's light into his hidden cave of shame. It was only there he could be fully loved, healed, transformed, and set free.

Jesus concluded by saying, "Peter, feed my sheep" (John 21:17). Here's my interpretation of what Jesus was saying. "Peter, I accept and love you, as you are. Now be your authentic self, and do what I called you to do."

The last thing Peter expected to encounter, wallowing in his cave of shame, was the forgiveness, healing, and love of Christ. Peter experienced the fullness of Jesus' love for him. His whole self, including his cowardice, was now brought into his relationship with Christ. He had no secrets left to hide. It was all out in the open and Jesus accepted him, as he was.

## 180 **Get a Hold of Yourself**

Peter understood he couldn't earn Jesus' love by giving the right answers, doing the right things, or being brave. Jesus loved him for who he was, including his contradictions—his courage and his cowardice.

We, too, can never experience being fully loved by God, until we bring our full selves into our relationship with God. Only the parts we expose to the light of God's presence can be healed, transformed, renewed, and loved. When we keep aspects of ourselves hidden, in the dark, suppressed and repressed, all we're doing is shutting out the healing light of God. This is why we need the cracks, the gaps our contradictions create in our lives. Because that's how the light gets in. The divine light of love.

We all have moments that reveal gaps in our identity. These moments can be mortifying. Perhaps you pride yourself on being a calm and rational person and lose your temper in a meeting. Or you're an outspoken environmentalist who gets called out for your high carbon footprint. Or you're admired by others for your honesty and integrity and get caught in a lie. Maybe you've worked hard to be a kind and fair parent, but in a moment of stress, you yell at your child for not putting the milk away, in front of company. Then someone reminds you, it was you who left it out.

These moments expose what our ego mind is obsessed with keeping concealed. Yet it's only when we stop trying to cover up these gaps in our identity, from others and ourselves, and face them, that we can fully experience God's unconditional love for who we are.

Nobody would have questioned Peter's courage and devotion to Jesus before his cowardly act of betrayal. Least of all himself. Now it seemed everyone was questioning it. Even Jesus. A gap, a contradiction had been revealed, and Jesus didn't want Peter to move past the gap too quickly. He let him sink into it, because he wanted Peter to understand that he loved who Peter was, not who Peter thought he needed to be.

After the third time Jesus asks, "Do you love me?," Peter is fully in the gap. He's never felt so low. He's completely sunk into his cavern of shame. It's there Jesus reminds him to do what he called him to do. Peter's failure, his cowardice, hasn't changed Jesus' love for him, and it hasn't changed Jesus' faith in him to be the spiritual leader he called him to be.

The things we're ashamed of are not what hinder us from being used by God. It's denying them, hiding them, fixating on them, or allowing them to define us, that hinder us from becoming our authentic self and being used by God.

This was a pivotal moment for Peter. He experienced the good news of Jesus in a fresh way, and experienced the healing, liberation, and renewal it brings. It was through this experience of accepting himself, with all his contradictions, that he was prepared for his spiritual awakening, the baptism of the Holy Spirit, which would occur a few days later. He was finally ready to walk in the Spirit, as his authentic self.

## WE KNOW, BY BEING KNOWN

Paul says, "To know fully, is to be fully known" (see 1 Corinthians 13:12). The only way to gain genuine insight, understanding, and wisdom is to let ourselves be fully known. Or to put it another way, our knowledge and understanding (especially of ourselves) is limited to the level we let ourselves be known. By God, first and foremost.

Jesus already knew Peter fully. He knew Peter would deny him and manifest his cowardice when the stakes got high enough. Yet Jesus knowing Peter is not what transformed

## 182  Get a Hold of Yourself

Peter. Peter had to let himself be known. He had to experience being fully known by Jesus. And that could only happen in his cave of shame. It was only then that Peter experienced being fully known, accepted, and loved by Jesus, as he was.

It's the same for us. God already knows you fully. God knows about your secret addictions, your vices, your vicious temper that only your family sees, the arrogance or prejudice you hide so well. It's only when you experience God knowing, accepting, and loving you fully, including the aspects you hide and are most ashamed of, that you're transformed, healed, and set free.

Paul says everything in our lives that we expose to God's light is not only healed and renewed, it becomes a light in the world (see Ephesians 5:13). It reflects the light of God's goodness and love to others. This can only happen after we accept our contradictions and enter these gaps in our lives, and let God meet us there.

## TWO STONES IN MY POCKET

A rabbi told me he always carried two stones with him, based on a Hasidic tradition he'd learned. He kept a blue stone in his right pocket that reminded him, "For my sake the world was created. I'm the apple of God's eye." In his left pocket he kept a slate stone that reminded him of another truth: "I am but dust and ashes. I'm an insignificant grain of sand on the shore of eternity." Multiple times a day he would reach in and take out whichever stone he needed in the moment. If he was feeling too proud or important, he took out the slate stone and held it. If he was feeling shame, despair, or hopeless, he took out the blue stone and held it. He would hold whichever stone he needed, for as long as he needed, until he was rebalanced in the whole truth, the paradoxical truth of his identity.

Since then, I've imagined I have two stones, representing the many contradictory truths in my life. For example, in my right pocket is an imaginary blue stone that reminds me, "I'm okay the way I am. I accept and love myself as I am." In my left pocket, an imaginary slate stone reminds me, "I'm not okay the way I am. I need to grow, change, and improve." I need both stones to keep me aware of my full contradictory self.

Jesus' path teaches us to live with both sides of the paradoxical truths in our lives and live in the tension this brings. We need the gaps they create, to open space in our lives to access the buried truths and hidden treasure. To experience God's love, acceptance, grace, and healing on deeper levels. To let our authentic self emerge.

## DOES THIS EXCUSE OUR BAD BEHAVIOR?

You may be wondering—what about our sinful contradictions? What if someone is generous to their friends and family but regularly steals from strangers. Or if someone is gentle and kind at work but abusive to his wife and children at home. Do these people simply need to embrace these contradictions in their lives?

It doesn't matter how extreme, sinful, or violent our contradictions are—the starting point of healing and growth is to acknowledge and accept them. Because they are truth. Only embracing the truth will set us free. To deny or resist the truth doesn't accomplish anything positive.

However, we must not stop there. To embrace our contradictions is to acknowledge the gap they create. We must enter the gap and intentionally invite the light of God's presence to meet us in the caves these gaps expose. This is necessary for our healing and transformation. Granted, some may not see the contradictions or gaps in their lives, or be indifferent to them. If your behavior causes harm to other people and you don't feel conflicted, guilt, or shame about this, you require a level of help and support this book cannot offer. For most of us, however, when we behave in sinful, destructive, or harmful ways, we feel conflicted, guilt, shame, or confusion. Most of us can sense the contradictions and gaps in our lives. At the very least, we sense a gap between who we are and who we should be, who we feel called to be, who we want to be. Embracing our contradictions isn't about excusing our bad behavior, it's the first step in the healing process of becoming our authentic self.

## THE SIX Es

I'm not a fan of formulas, but breaking down the process of becoming our authentic self into steps might be helpful.

1. Engage the paradoxical teachings and principles of Jesus, to help us grow in self-awareness.
2. Experience the cycle of death and rebirth, of losing ourselves to find ourselves.
3. Embrace the contradictions in our lives.
4. Explore what's underneath the gaps these contradictions create in our identities.
5. Expose our full, complicated, and contradictory self to the light of God.
6. Emerge—let our essential self of awareness emerge and become our center.

## PUTTING THE SIX Es TO WORK

Let's consider a common contradiction, such as greed and generosity, to illustrate how these six Es work. Here's how these steps have brought healing, freedom, and authenticity in my own struggle with being greedy and generous.

1.  As I engaged Jesus' teachings, they challenged me to be honest about my greed as well as my generosity.
2.  I experienced death to self as I let go of my identity of being only a generous person, surrendering the generous persona I projected to the world.
3.  I trusted Jesus' claim that the truth would set me free and embraced the truth of this contradiction in my life.
4.  I explored what was underneath the gap of this contradiction fully, without judgment.
5.  I exposed the contradiction of my greed and generosity to God and invited the Spirit into my struggle to accept and understand this aspect of myself.
6.  As I experienced God's love, healing, and wisdom in my cave of greed, my essential self emerged and became the center of my consciousness.

Let me unpack steps 5 and 6 in more detail.

When I invited the Spirit into the gap created by my greed and generosity, not only did I feel God's unconditional love for me, I gained understanding and insight into my greed. Remember, our understanding and insight about our authentic self is limited to the level we let ourselves be known by God.

The Spirit helped me see my greed was rooted in a scarcity mentality. A belief there's not enough. That if I don't get my piece of the pie as quickly and aggressively as possible, there will be no pie left for me. I became aware of childhood experiences that planted and nurtured this belief in my life.

As I continued to invite the Spirit into my inner depths, the Spirit planted, watered, and nourished seeds of abundance in

## 186  Get a Hold of Yourself

my mind and heart. I began to see the reality of abundance. I began to see and believe there's always enough, when God is with me. And thankfully, God is always with me, even when I mess up and act greedily.

God also revealed a great deal of my generosity was my ego mind attempting to project and protect my preferred self-image. I was often being generous for selfish reasons, to be liked, respected, and admired. My generosity wasn't always helpful to myself or the recipients of my generosity, because my motivation was to be rewarded. To get something out of it.

As I continued to expose this gap to God, the Spirit continued to help me understand how I could be both generous and greedy in a healthy way. I learned my greed is ultimately rooted in the belief that I deserve goodness, fulfillment, joy, and peace as a child of God. However, I learned the treasure I'm truly seeking won't come by accumulating as much of the pie as I can get my hands on, because the fruit of the Spirit is the treasure I really desire. And these will only increase in my life as I walk in the Spirit.

I now understand God isn't trying to eliminate my greed but redeem, heal, and transform it. Greed is essentially the desire for more, and there's nothing wrong with desiring more truth, love, justice, peace, joy, and freedom. My greed is rooted in a desire to live the best and highest quality of life possible, and that's not wrong. How I act upon this desire, however, is where I often get into trouble. Thankfully, God is transforming how I understand, experience, and act upon it.

As a result, my "greed," or my *wanting*, has a new target. It's aimed at a life filled with the fruit of the Spirit. A life that's aimed at God's best for me, and for all of humanity and creation. This is freeing me to live as my authentic self, to walk in the Spirit, without denying my greed or my generosity.

## THE STRUGGLE WITHIN US

The struggle between greed and generosity is only one of many issues I wrestle with. However, all my struggles can be boiled down to one primary struggle. My struggle to walk in the Spirit consistently.

Walking in the Spirit is to live in the awareness of our oneness with God and in harmony with God's Spirit within us. It's a struggle to live this way because there are other powers at work in us. Paul talks a lot about this internal power struggle for control of our consciousness. In Romans 7, where Paul admits that what he wants to do he does *not* do, and vice versa, he shares some profound insight about this internal struggle. I'd encourage you to read the chapter, especially verses 15–25, but here's my summary of what he says.

1. Our inner beings are so complex, we can't fully understand ourselves or why we behave the way we do.
2. There are different powers at work within us, in conflict with one another.
3. Our essential self never acts contrary to God's ways. Our essential self always loves God and is always in harmony with God's laws.
4. When we act in ways that are contrary to God, our essential self is no longer in charge, it's the result of another power taking over.

Paul admits he can't live the life he wants to live, because there's a power within him that takes over. In Romans 7 he calls this power *sin*. Sin comes from the Greek word *hamartia*, meaning to miss the mark or the intended target. The target or goal is walking in the Spirit. Sin is whatever causes us to deviate from this.

## *188* **Get a Hold of Yourself**

## *SARX* VERSUS SPIRIT

Paul refers to this internal struggle most often as a battle between *sarx* and the Spirit. The Greek word *sarx* is usually translated into the English word *flesh*. Flesh typically has a neutral or positive meaning in the Bible, usually referring to the physical body or body parts of humans and animals. Bible dictionaries offer an additional definition for *sarx*, however, that is negative and implies a spiritual quality more than a physical one. The negative definition of *sarx* is an energy that resists and is adversarial to God and God's will. *Sarx* is a power within us, that resists harmony with the Spirit.

If we look at a few passages from Paul's writings, using the word *sarx* instead of the word *flesh*, we see what Paul is getting at.

> Those who live according to the *sarx* have their minds set on what the *sarx* desires; but those who live in accordance with the Spirit have their minds set on what the Spirit desires. The mind governed by the *sarx* is death, but the mind governed by the Spirit is life and peace. The mind governed by the *sarx* is hostile to God; it does not submit to God's law, nor can it do so. Those who are in the realm of the *sarx* cannot please God. (Romans 8:5–8)

We see the battle between *sarx* and the Spirit is a struggle for control of our mind, our consciousness. Paul says we must choose which power we will walk in and let govern our consciousness.

In his letter to the church in Galatia, Paul writes,

> So I say, walk by the Spirit, and you will not gratify the desires of the *sarx*. For the *sarx* desires what is contrary to

the Spirit, and the Spirit what is contrary to the *sarx*. They are in conflict with each other. (Galatians 5:16–17)

Paul isn't saying we will desire different things, depending on whether we're walking in the Spirit or *sarx*. Not necessarily. He's saying the way desires manifest in our lives will be different. We'll experience and fulfill these desires in different ways. Contrary ways.

For example, we'll experience hunger, whether we're walking in the Spirit or *sarx*. As humans, we need to eat. What will be different and contrary is the way the desire of hunger is experienced, processed, and fulfilled. Paul's not telling us to do away with our bodily desires, like hunger, but to bring them into alignment with the desires of the Spirit.

In a state of *sarx* consciousness, our eating is aimed only at satisfying the urge, fulfilling the desire. When we're in the Spirit, our eating aims to be in harmony with God and God's best, meaning what is best for us and all the lives involved in providing and preparing the food we eat. *Sarx* just wants to taste the flavor, experience pleasure, satiate the hunger, numb the pain, or temporarily fill an inner void. In the Spirit, we care about where our food comes from, how it impacts the environment and other people, and how it nourishes our body, as well as our mind, heart, and soul. This is why many spiritual people are conscious and contentious eaters. They might choose a vegan or vegetarian diet, or intentionally eat locally and sustainably, or say a prayer of thanksgiving before meals. They recognize it's important to stop, pause, and reflect on the epic journey this food has taken to become our meal, and thank the life that gives us life. To thank the ultimate source of all our food, the Creator of the universe. In the

190   **Get a Hold of Yourself**

Spirit, our eating is present, grateful, and mindful of how our eating impacts others, our cities, nation, animals, rivers, trees, and planet.

In short, the way our hunger is experienced, processed, and fulfilled will be different, often contrary, to how we eat when *sarx* is in control.

## EMBRACING THE STRUGGLE

Walking in the Spirit is easy, in theory. I understand how to do it. Yet I find myself continually struggling to do it. I'm constantly oscillating between walking in the Spirit and walking in the *sarx*. For most of us, this will be an ongoing struggle, as it was for Paul. If you're struggling in your faith, in your spiritual journey, you're not alone.

One of the ways we tend to amplify this struggle, however, is by struggling with the struggle. At some point, we need to embrace the struggle, as part of God's process. According to Scripture, seasons of suffering, adversity, and struggle are necessary and valuable. I'm not saying this applies to all suffering on earth. (To address the existence of all suffering in the world is beyond the scope of this book and my intellect.) However, I've come to understand how this truth applies to my own life. Suffering and struggle have value because I need them to grow.

I'm not saying God causes bad things to happen to us, so we'll grow. I'm saying God can use whatever happens to us to help us grow. The greatest fertilizer for growth is often the manure that happens to us. But we must take what happens, and how it's impacting us, and release it into God's hands, trusting God can make something good of it. As we live this way, we see God can redeem our suffering and struggle. (*Redeem* means to compensate for the faults or bad aspects of something.)

**Authenticity** *191*

Paul says, "We rejoice in our sufferings, because suffering produces endurance, and endurance produces character" (see Romans 5:3–4). James says, "We should consider it pure joy when we face trials and tribulations, because the testing of our faith produces perseverance" (see James 1:2–3).

It might seem like strange advice, to rejoice when we suffer and struggle. But what Paul and James are saying is that certain traits and qualities, like patience, resilience, perseverance, and courage, primarily grow in us as we go through suffering, adversity, and struggle. If we prioritize growth in our lives, we'll not only value these tough seasons, we'll rejoice in them. Not because our faith is masochistic, but because our faith enables us to see they're producing beneficial fruit in our lives.

Twenty years ago, a Zimbabwean pastor told me, "One thing I've learned about North American Christians is you don't like to suffer or be uncomfortable." At the time I thought, "What a strange thing to say. Who likes to suffer?" I've come to realize he was right. Our contemporary North American mindset seems obsessed with eliminating suffering and avoiding hardship at all costs. This has undermined our trust in the divine wisdom that says suffering, adversity, and trials are necessary and valuable, because we cannot grow and become our authentic self without them.

Several years ago, I was going through a difficult time. I met with one of my mentors, named Dave. I said, "Dave, I'm really struggling." His response surprised me. "That's good. Struggle is a sign of life. When the fish on the end of your line is struggling, that means it wants to live and be free. It's the same with us. None of us are perfect. We all have stuff we're struggling with. If we aren't, we're either spiritually asleep or we've given up."

Dave's feedback helped me realize that to value growth is to be grateful for the process that leads to growth. Which

*192* **Get a Hold of Yourself**

includes struggle. I began practicing gratitude for adversity, struggle, and suffering, trusting God would use them to produce growth in me. Eventually.

In Galatians, Paul says, "Do not grow weary in doing good and being faithful, for we will reap a harvest in due season, if we don't lose heart. If we don't give up" (Galatians 6:9, my paraphrase). There will be seasons when we struggle and can't see anything good coming from it. When we suffer and see no rhyme or reason for it. When we put in the hard work, without seeing results. When we're doing what we ought to be doing, without reaping the fruit of our labors. When this happens, in our careers, marriages, parenting, friendships, spiritual growth, or any other area of life, it's discouraging. Human beings are designed to be fueled by progress. It's tempting to slack off or give up when we're not seeing results. Yet having faith not only means continuing to be faithful to God, it means trusting God will be faithful to us. Trusting that in due season, we will reap a harvest. If we don't give up. Eventually the struggle and suffering will bear fruit, if we endure.

## WRESTLING WITH GOD

There's a story in the Bible about a peculiar wrestling match between Jacob and a mysterious stranger (Genesis 32:22–32). The passage says they wrestled all night. As dawn approaches, his wrestling opponent sees Jacob is not going to stop battling with him. So he dislocates Jacob's hip. Jacob finally sees he can't win. Exhausted and wounded, Jacob realizes he's done. Then he does something surprising. Instead of giving up, he grabs hold of his wrestling opponent and says, "I will not let you go, I will not give up, even though I know I can't win, until you bless me." That's when an even bigger twist is revealed in the story. It turns out Jacob's wrestling opponent is God. God responds by blessing Jacob, saying, "Your name will no longer be Jacob, but Israel, because you have struggled with God and with humans and have overcome" (see 32:28).

One of the questions this story raises for me is, why did God say Jacob prevailed in his struggle with God? Jacob didn't win this wrestling match.

In God's eyes, to overcome or prevail doesn't always mean you defeat what you're struggling with. It means you don't give up. Jacob persisted. He refused to give up, even when it was obvious he couldn't win. He overcame when he embraced what he was struggling with and sought a blessing in it. This is how we can overcome as well. When we embrace our struggle and seek a blessing in it.

The blessing Jacob receives is God revealing his divine calling and true identity. By embracing his struggle, Jacob was released from his burdened past, guilt, and shame, and his authentic self emerged. The same is true for us. As we embrace our struggle, we're often blessed with greater insight into our authentic self and purpose.

As I've learned to seek a blessing in my struggle, it's profoundly changed my quality of life. I'm able to trust that God still loves me, is still available to me, and is pouring peace, joy, wisdom, and creativity into my life, even when I struggle to walk in the Spirit. This didn't make sense to my thirty-five-year-old self, who was determined to walk in the Spirit perfectly, if I could only discipline myself more. Yet this paradoxical life of growth and grace is my reality now, in my fifties. And it's beyond liberating.

However, notice Jacob's blessing also came with a wound. A wound that slowed him down and stayed with him for the rest of his life. When we persist and refuse to give up, we eventually see we cannot win. The struggle of life is beyond us. The

*194* **Get a Hold of Yourself**

struggle to be perfect is futile. The struggle to comprehensively and clearly understand life, God, other people, and ourselves is impossible. Yet if we stop struggling with our struggle, and embrace it, then what happened for Jacob eventually happens for us. We receive a blessing. At the very least, the blessing of Immanuel. The awareness that God is with us, even when we're struggling.

But we'll probably walk away from this moment of clarity with a limp, alongside the blessing. Becoming our authentic self almost always comes with wounds. For instance, God has blessed me with the realization that life isn't worth living without love. To love is to risk being hurt, taken advantage of, used. To love is to make ourselves vulnerable. We will all incur wounds on the path of Jesus. God's promise is that we'll also receive blessings on this path.

## WE SURRENDER TO WIN

Living as our authentic self involves struggle. We don't become awakened, saved, or filled with the Spirit and then magically live as our authentic self for the rest of our days, living happily ever after. That's not how this works. The paradox of spiritual growth is that we're not set free *from* the struggle of life, but *through* it. We're not liberated from suffering, but through it. We don't always overcome by winning, but by surrendering.

Ego mind clings to the illusion of control; the essential self surrenders to "what is," trusting God is good and will lead us to God's best, through whatever happens. When we understand this, we stop labeling struggle, suffering, and surrender as negative things to be avoided or eliminated from our lives. We see they can have value. That they're not preventing us from enjoying life—they're an integral part of life, helping us to awaken and live authentically.

# CONCLUSION

Your authentic self is like a unique stained glass window, bearing a one-of-a-kind image of God. There's no stained glass window quite like yours, anywhere in history. When your authentic self is illuminated, you bring a unique blessing into the world. You make this planet a better, more interesting and beautiful place. However, the only way your stained glass window fully shines is by letting the Christ light within you illuminate it.

When we're spiritually awakened, we know who we are in Christ. We're aware of our oneness with God. When we live in this awareness and walk in the Spirit, we're no longer trying to figure out who we are or our place, status, purpose or significance in the world. What matters now is focusing on the Christ light within us, and letting it shine through our unique stained glass window.

It's when our authentic self shines that we most effectively love God, others, and ourselves. When we live and act in ways that energize and utilize the fullness of our unique set of gifts, skills, experiences, personality, passion, and traits, while being aware of our oneness with God and everyone around us.

## 196 Get a Hold of Yourself

However, letting our authentic self shine requires forgetting or losing ourselves. To stop focusing on ourselves.

## TO KNOW YOURSELF IS TO FORGET YOURSELF

For decades, I was focused on self-improvement, self-healing, and self-development. Driven to know and become the ideal person I thought God expected me to be. With God's help, I made a lot of progress in many areas over the years. This was an important part of my growth journey, and it produced much fruit. Yet no matter how much progress I made, I inevitably became aware of more things to work on. Not only that, some of the stuff I thought I'd dealt with or had been healed from in the past resurfaced. The quest to be my ideal self seemed impossible.

Ten years ago, I shared this struggle with my Trappist monk spiritual director. He told me, "Troy, the only question God will ask you when you get to heaven is this. Were you—you?" He paused, then added, "I hate to break it to you, but you're not perfect. You'll never be perfect. You're not the ideal pastor. You're you. So *be* you."

He helped me see my quest to become the ideal Troy was keeping my focus on myself. I was fixated on my identity and who I needed to be. I was spending too much time on my own, in introspective reflection, reading my Bible, praying, meditating, repenting, and studying, and not enough time with family, church members, friends, and people in my community. I was so focused on growing spiritually, I was neglecting my neighbors. I was failing to be present, to love others, and to let my light shine, because I was determined to perfect my stained glass window before allowing the Christ light within me to shine through it.

I finally came to understand the gospel of Jesus that says our oneness with God and our usefulness to God isn't something we attain by becoming sinless. It's not something we earn or accomplish with our growth. It's not who we will be when we're perfect, because of our hard work, sacrifice, and faith. It's based on who we already are "in Christ." It's a current reality that God has established through Jesus' life, death, and resurrection, and that God makes us aware of by God's Spirit. When we experience this reality, we're no longer focused on ourselves. All the energy directed inward to change, fix, heal, and improve ourselves is invested outward into the world— to bless, serve, support, and love others. Because we're no longer fussing over our contradictions, issues, shortcomings, and imperfections.

The gospel of Jesus grounds us in God's free gift of grace, liberating us from the need to change to measure up. It gets our eyes off ourselves. Which paradoxically sets us free to grow and change. The twentieth-century psychiatrist Carl Rogers put it this way: "The curious paradox is that when I accept myself just as I am, then I can change."[1] The best way to grow is by accepting God's grace and accepting ourselves as we are while staying aware of our oneness with God and letting the Christ light within us shine through our imperfect stained glass windows.

## FEEL GOD'S PLEASURE IN WHO YOU ARE

The stained glass window of our authentic self is never finished. It's a unique piece of art we continue to co-create with God's Spirit as we journey through life. But the only way our authentic self shines beauty and God's light into this world is when we allow the Christ light within us—who we are in

*198* **Get a Hold of Yourself**

Christ—to shine through it. We do this by staying grounded in our essential self and walking in the Spirit. This requires repenting when we miss the mark, but it doesn't require groveling or penance. To repent means to reorient the focus of our awareness onto God's presence within us. It's acknowledging when we're identifying with ego mind or *sarx* and then choosing to ground our awareness in our oneness with God, "Christ in us." When we do this, our authentic self shines. And this is what pleases God.

Eric Liddell, the Scottish Olympic runner portrayed in the movie *Chariots of Fire*, said, "When I run, I feel God's pleasure." When we shine as our authentic self, we bring God pleasure. Unlike Eric Liddell, I don't shine when I run. My running might amuse God and those around me, but it's not when I shine. I usually shine when I'm creating or playing music, preaching, writing, or bantering with a group of friends, making them laugh. Certain activities make me come alive and radiate with my brightest light. That animated energy I'm experiencing in those moments is God's joy, God taking pleasure in me—the artwork God created. God loves it when his art shines.

Other people pick up on it when we're authentic. They sense the shine. You've probably sensed this in your own life. It might be when you're cooking, gardening, playing with children, solving problems, repairing an engine, dancing, leading a team meeting. Whatever it is, we all have a shine. Something that makes us feel alive and whole, where we enter a state of flow. When we're spiritually awakened, we feel God's pleasure when we shine. Like Eric Liddell felt when he ran.

What makes you light up? What makes you forget about yourself and be fully present in the flow, in the moment? What makes you feel God's pleasure? These are glimpses of your authentic self. Of how God expects you—God's unique piece of art—to shine in the world.

The reason God created you the way you are is for you to be you. And your contradictions, struggles, and limitations are part of what makes you "you." Along with your gifts, abilities, and passion. Shining your authentic self is how you best love and serve the world, others, and God. When you do what only you can do, as you are, and as you continue to grow.

So shine on friends. This world needs more light.

# NOTES

## CHAPTER 1

1. E. C. Gaze, "Debunking the Dunning-Kruger Effect—The Least Skilled People Know How Much They Don't Know, but Everyone Thinks They Are Better Than Average," The Conversation, May 12, 2023, https://theconversation.com/debunking-the-dunning-kruger-effect-the-least-skilled-people-know-how-much-they-dont-know-but-everyone-thinks-they-are-better-than-average-195527.

2. Tasha Eurich, "What Self-Awareness Really Is (and How to Cultivate It)," *Harvard Business Review* 4, no. 4 (2018): 1–9, quoted in Jeff Kauflin, "Only 15% of People Are Self-Aware—Here's How to Change," *Forbes*, February 20, 2024, https://www.forbes.com/sites/jeffkauflin/2017/05/10/only-15-of-people-are-self-aware-heres-how-to-change/.

3. Anthony de Mello, *Awareness Conversations with the Masters* (Image, 1990), 5.

4. bell hooks, "bell hooks and John Perry Barlow Talk 'Prana in Cyberspace,'" *Lion's Roar*, December 13, 2023, https://www.lionsroar.com/bell-hooks-talks-to-john-perry-barlow/.

5. A modern translation of a statement written by J. B. S. Haldane in an essay entitled "Possible Worlds." The original quote, "The universe is not only queerer than we suppose, but queerer than we can suppose," was reprinted in Haldane, *Possible Worlds and Other Essays* (Chatto and Windus, 1927), 286.

6. Neil Degrasse Tyson, *Astrophysics for People in a Hurry* (W. W. Norton, 2017), 13.

7. C. G. Jung, *Collected Works of C. G. Jung, Volume 12: Psychology and Alchemy*, ed. Gerhard Adler and R. F. C. Hull (Princeton University Press, 1968), 18.

8. Jung, *Collected Works of C. G. Jung, Volume 11: Psychology and Religion: West and East*, ed. Adler and Hull (Princeton University Press: 1969), 417.

9. Charles Spurgeon, *Feeding On the Bread of Life*, vol. 46, Sermon #2706, https://www.spurgeongems.org/sermon/chs2706.pdf.

## CHAPTER 2

1. Jeremiah S. Chechik, director, *National Lampoon's Christmas Vacation* (Warner Bros., 1989).

2. Jason T. Newsom, Nathalie Huguet et al., "Health Behavior Change Following Chronic Illness in Middle and Later Life," *Journals of Gerontology*, series B, vol. 67B, no. 3 (May 2012): 279–88, https://doi.org/10.1093/geronb/gbr103.

## 202 Get a Hold of Yourself

### CHAPTER 3

1. Malcolm Gladwell, "Choice, Happiness and Spaghetti Sauce," TED Talk, https://www.ted.com/talks/malcolm_gladwell_choice_happiness_and_spaghetti_sauce.
2. Daniel Ladinsky, trans., *Love Poems from God: Twelve Sacred Voices from East and West* (Penguin, 2002), 85.
3. *The Simpsons*, season 8, ep. 12., dir. Mark Kirkland, written by John Swartzwelder. Originally aired on Fox in the United States, February 2, 1997.
4. Joseph Campbell quoted in Maureen Stearns, *Conscious Courage: Turning Everyday Challenges into Opportunities* (Enrichment Books, 2004), 15.

### CHAPTER 4

1. Maya Angelou, *I Know Why the Caged Bird Sings* (Random House, 2010), 264.
2. Father António da Ascenção, trans. Rev. Carlos A. Martins.
3. Marcus Aurelius, *Meditations*, trans. Martin Hammond (Penguin Pocket Hardbacks, Penguin Classics, 2014), 2.11.
4. Plato, *Phaedo* (Clarendon Press, 1911), Section 64a.

### CHAPTER 5

1. William Shakespeare, *Hamlet*, ed. Barbara Mowat, Paul Werstine et al. (Folger Shakespeare Library, n.d.), 1.3.84. References are to act, scene, and line. https://www.folger.edu/explore/shakespeares-works/hamlet/read/.
2. Tony Robbins, "Become a Master of Influence," https://www.tonyrobbins.com/career-business/become-a-master-of-influence/.
3. Kazimierz Dąbrowski (1902–1980) was a Polish psychologist, psychiatrist, and physician best known for his theory of "positive disintegration" (TPD). You can read more about his theory in his books *Personal Disintegration* and *Personality-Shaping Through Positive Disintegration*.
4. Toni Morrison, *Beloved* (Knopf, 1991), 234.
5. Rachel Held Evans, *Searching for Sunday: Loving, Leaving, and Finding the Church* (Thomas Nelson Inc., 2015), 19.

### CHAPTER 6

1. Olivia Crist and Julia Willoughby Nason, dirs., *Shiny Happy People: Duggar Family Secrets*, Amazon Studios, 2023, https://www.amazon.com/Shiny-Happy-People-Duggar-Secrets/dp/B0B8TR2QV5.
2. Jeff Chu and Sarah Bessey, hosts, "Episode 5: Welcome to the Wilderness with Sarah Bessey," *Evolving Faith* (podcast), September 22, 2020, https://evolvingfaith.com/podcast/season-1/episode-5.
3. T. S. Eliot, *Four Quartets* (Harcourt, Brace, 1943).
4. Ḥāfiẓ, *The Gift: Poems by Hafiz*, trans. Daniel James Ladinsky (Penguin Compass, 1999), 203.
5. Brené Brown mentions this in the introductions of two of her books: *The Gifts of Imperfection: Let Go of Who You Think You're Supposed to Be and Embrace Who You Are* (Hazelden Publishing, 2010) and *Daring Greatly: How the Courage to Be Vulnerable Transforms the Way We Live, Love, Parent, and Lead* (Baker & Taylor, 2012).

**Notes** *203*

## CHAPTER 7

1. "A Murder a Minute," CBS News, October 3, 2002, https://www.cbsnews.com/news/a-murder-a-minute/.
2. Jan W. Van Strien and Lynne A. Isbell, "Snake Scales, Partial Exposure, and the Snake Detection Theory: A Human Event-Related Potentials Study," *Nature News*, April 7, 2017, https://www.nature.com/articles/srep46331.
3. "European Viper," *Encyclopædia Britannica*, https://www.britannica.com/animal/European-viper.
4. Betty Grayson and Morris I. Stein, "Attracting Assault: Victim's Nonverbal Cues," *Journal of Communication* 31, no. 1 (2006): 68–75, https://doi.org/10.1111/j.1460-2466.1981.tb01206.x.
5. Grayson and Stein.

## CHAPTER 8

1. Søren Kierkegaard, "Despair Is the Sickness unto Death," in *Kierkegaard's Writings, XIX, Vol. 19: Sickness Unto Death: A Christian Psychological Exposition for Upbuilding and Awakening*, ed. Howard V. Hong and Edna H. Hong (Princeton University Press, 1980), 13–21.
2. David Richo, *How to Be an Adult* (Paulist Press, 1991), 3.
3. Richard C. Schwartz, *No Bad Parts: Healing Trauma and Restoring Wholeness* (Vermilion, 2021), 98

## CHAPTER 9

1. Elizabeth Barrett Browning, *Aurora Leigh* (Chapman and Hall, 1857), book 7, line 821.

## CHAPTER 10

1. This story is often referred to as the "Cherokee Tale of Two Wolves." Its origin is unknown, but it is commonly attributed to various Indigenous peoples of North America, most frequently the Cherokee.
2. You can read the full story in Matthew 26:33–35; Mark 14:29–31; Luke 22:31–38; and John 13:37–38.

## CONCLUSION

1. Carl R. Rogers, *On Becoming a Person: A Therapist's View of Psychotherapy* (Houghton Mifflin, 1961), 17.

# THE AUTHOR

Troy D. Watson is a Mennonite pastor, columnist, and music recording artist. He writes and speaks on issues of spiritual and personal growth from a theological and psychological perspective. His columns have appeared in the *Canadian Mennonite*, the *St. Catharines Standard*, and Sun Media publications. Watson resides in Stratford, Ontario, with his wife Tammy and his two sons Elias and Cai.